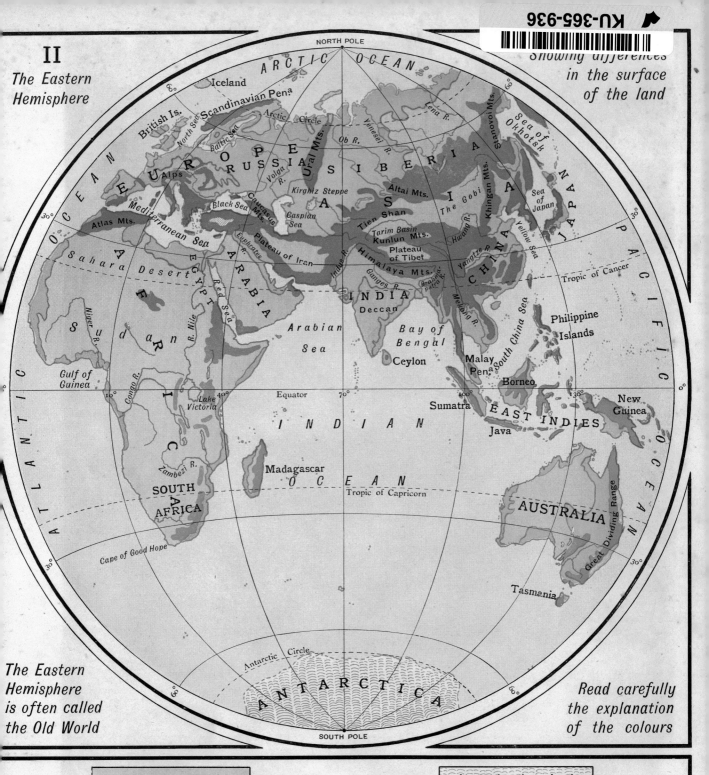

II
The Eastern Hemisphere

Showing differences in the surface of the land

The Eastern Hemisphere is often called the Old World

Read carefully the explanation of the colours

Map labels:

NORTH POLE

ARCTIC OCEAN

Iceland · British Is. · Scandinavian Pen. · North Sea · Baltic Sea · Arctic Circle · Ural Mts. · Ob R. · Yenesei R. · Lena R. · Stanovoi Mts. · Sea of Okhotsk

EUROPE · RUSSIA · SIBERIA · JAPAN · Sea of Japan

Alps · Caucasus Mts. · Volga R. · Kirghiz Steppe · Altai Mts. · The Gobi · Khingan Mts. · Yellow Sea

Atlas Mts. · Mediterranean Sea · Black Sea · Caspian Sea · Tien Shan · Kunlun Mts. · Tarim Basin · Huang R. · Yangtze R. · CHINA

Sahara Desert · AFRICA · EGYPT · ARABIA · Plateau of Iran · Euphrates · Indus R. · Plateau of Tibet · Himalaya Mts. · Ganges R. · Brahmaputra · Mekong R. · Tropic of Cancer

Niger R. · R. Nile · Red Sea · Sudan · INDIA · Deccan · Arabian Sea · Bay of Bengal · Ceylon · Malay Pen. · South China Sea · Philippine Islands · Borneo

Gulf of Guinea · Congo R. · Lake Victoria · Equator · Sumatra · EAST INDIES · Java · New Guinea

INDIAN OCEAN

Zambezi R. · Madagascar · Tropic of Capricorn · AUSTRALIA

SOUTH AFRICA · Cape of Good Hope · Great Dividing Range · Tasmania

ATLANTIC OCEAN · PACIFIC OCEAN

Antarctic Circle · ANTARCTICA

SOUTH POLE

Plateaus and Hilly Lands

For the most part, plateaus and hilly lands have a rougher surface than plains, but are not such rough lands as mountains. A few of the plateaus are very high, while some of the hilly lands are rather low.

Lands buried under Snow and Ice

These are cold, frozen lands of the Far North and the Far South. They lie under a thick covering of snow and ice which never melts away.

GEOGRAPHY
FIRST SERIES

BY

A. B. ARCHER, M.A.
Head Master, Oldershaw School for Boys, Wallasey

AND

HELEN G. THOMAS

BOOK FOUR

GINN AND COMPANY LTD.
QUEEN SQUARE, LONDON, W.C.1

CONTENTS

I. *A SPRING DAY*

	PAGE
1. In the North Woods . .	5
2. In London	8

II. *ANTARCTICA—THE FROZEN CONTINENT*

1. Some Brave Explorers . .	13
2. Why Antarctica is so Cold .	15
3. The Loneliest Land . . .	18

III. *THE NOMAD LANDS*

1. Exploring with Globes and Maps	21
2. The Far North and its Wandering Peoples . . .	25
The Reindeer Lands . . .	25
The Eskimos of the American Tundra	30
Why the Far North has so few People	34
3. The Steppes and Deserts .	35
The Wandering Kirghiz . .	35
The Greatest Stretch of Dry Lands	40
The Oases and their People .	42

IV. *LANDS OF SCATTERED SETTLEMENTS*

1. More about the Dry Lands .	47
2. The Northern Forests . .	50
Lands too Cool for Farming .	50
Fur-Trappers and their Work .	52
Mill Towns and Logging Camps	56
Some Things to Remember about the Northern Forests . .	59

	PAGE
3. The Tropical Forests . .	62
Map Discoveries	62
A Trip up the Amazon River .	63
A Day with a Rubber-Gatherer	66
The Congo Forest . . .	68
Why the Tropical Forests are not Thickly Populated . . .	70
4. The Mountainous Lands .	73
Some Cool Lands within the Tropics	74
A Glimpse of the Rocky Mountains	76
Why the Settlements in Mountainous Lands are Scattered .	77

V. *THE CROWDED LANDS*

1. The Orient and India . .	81
Japan and its Tiny Farms . .	82
Glimpses of China . . .	87
Java and its Plantations . .	90
India—Land of Contrasts . .	95
2. The Crowded Part of the New World	101
America's Busy Cities . .	102
American Farms, Forests, and Mines	105
3. Ourselves and Our European Neighbours	112
Britain—A Story of Changes .	112
Glimpses of the Continent . .	116
4. Some Things to Remember about the Crowded Lands	122

GENERAL QUESTIONS . . .	123
INDEX	127

203607

Printed in Great Britain by R. & R. CLARK, LIMITED, *Edinburgh*

FOREWORD

THIS book is the fourth of a series of four text-books designed to introduce children to geography in a friendly, informal way, and to put at their disposal a means of discovering the simpler geographic facts and relationships.

In all the books the emphasis is on people —how they live and why they live as they do. There is no parade of factual material to be memorized ; no attempt to build up a series of books which will fit nicely into the arid " formal development " of a happily out-moded day. On the contrary, the authors use the story-book method to bring into juxtaposition facts of geography and facts of human life and activities between which the pupils can clearly discern the relationships. In short, the books expose the children to the stimulating contagion of learning, rather than impose upon them the dull routine of being taught.

Pictures play a vital part in each book. They have been selected and prepared, not as mere embellishments of the pages, but as definite visual aids to learning. The globes and maps have a similar function. Confusion of names has been rigidly avoided, each globe or map carrying only the data necessary for its particular objective. There are no formal map studies of the type which, from a child's point of view, have no *raison d'être*. Wherever in the course of the text a globe or map can contribute to the learning process, directions or suggestions for using it are given in a guise which transforms the children into explorers and the map studies into adventures in discovery.

This fourth book of the series is designed to give pupils their first acquaintance with the world as a whole. It serves to round out the first elementary study of geography, and to provide a foundation for the work of subsequent years.

As a main theme for the book the authors have chosen the most significant single fact of human geography — the extraordinarily uneven distribution of people over the face of the earth. With this fact as a *motif*, the text carries pupils far and wide in its descriptions of human life and activities as related to varying conditions of physical environment.

Touching here and there on lands in all continents and in varying latitudes, the book is broad in scope, but by no means comprehensive. On the contrary, it is definitely and purposely selective. Each country or region described has been chosen because it exemplifies a certain combination of geographic conditions which, more or less, control population density and dictate a certain mode of life.

The teacher will not expect the year's work to result in a detailed knowledge of the geography of the world. He will be satisfied if his pupils gain an elementary understanding of human-geographic relationships and an interest in geography great enough to whet the appetite for more.

A. B. ARCHER
H. G. THOMAS

A Canadian fur-trapper and his dog-team

CHAPTER ONE

A SPRING DAY

1. IN THE NORTH WOODS

LET us pretend that it is spring, and that we are in the great North Woods of Canada. All through the winter this land of trees, lakes, and streams has lain under a blanket of soft snow. The lonely cabins, scattered along the frozen streams, have been half buried in snow-drifts piled up by the cold north wind.

Now the snow has melted, and the racing streams sparkle in the spring sunshine. The dark evergreen trees have lost their winter caps of snow and have put on their spring trimming of pale green shoots. The new leaves on the birch trees rustle softly in the morning breeze.

Round a bend in one of the rivers comes a canoe. A young man sits in the stern, driving the little boat forward with swift, silent strokes of his paddle. The young man is a French-Canadian, and his name is Baptiste.

Three days have passed since Baptiste said good-bye to his wife and baby in the little log cabin far up the river. Three days of steady paddling have brought him nearly a hundred and fifty miles from home, yet in all that distance he has passed only two or three little villages along the river.

Here and there Baptiste has seen a lonely cabin like his own, but nowhere has he seen a farmhouse or

By courtesy of Canadian National Railways
A trapper on his snow-shoes in the woods

a farmer ploughing land for crops. For miles and miles the river winds through woods where not a house of any kind is to be found.

Each night Baptiste camps out on the river-bank. As soon as he has pulled his canoe ashore, he cuts some small branches and twigs from an evergreen tree and spreads them on the ground for his bed. Then he builds a fire and sets about cooking his supper. He has some salt pork with him, and some flour for making biscuits.

After supper he sits for some time with his back against a tree, smoking his pipe, listening to the murmur of the water, and watching the twinkling stars. Then he rolls up in a blanket and goes to sleep on his bed of evergreens.

You or I might be lonely or afraid in this great wilderness of trees. But Baptiste was born in the North Woods, and he is used to living in the quiet forest with only the wild animals for neighbours. He is never lonely or afraid.

By sunrise, Baptiste is up and on his way again. To-day, before the sun sets, he will pull his canoe out of the water at a trading-station on the shore of Hudson Bay. Then we shall see what he has in those big bundles which he has brought from home.

Perhaps you have guessed that Baptiste is a fur-trapper. He spends the long, cold winter trapping foxes and other wild animals whose thick-furred pelts, or skins, will bring a good price at the trading-station. He sets his traps at different places in the woods for several miles round his cabin.

Every few days, unless the weather is too stormy, Baptiste leaves the cabin with a sledge drawn by his team of dogs. He wears snow-shoes so that he can walk over the snow without sinking in.

Baptiste goes to one trap after another. He kills the animals that have been caught and brings them home on his sledge. On some trips he gets a good many animals, and on others only a few. But during the long, snowy winter he usually

A Canadian fur-trading station like the one where Baptiste sells his pelts

traps enough animals to make a good canoe-load of pelts to take down the river to the trading-station in the spring.

All through the winter Baptiste seldom sees anyone but his own family. His nearest neighbour, a trapper like himself, lives several miles away. The nearest village, where he can get his letters and buy supplies, is so far away that it takes Baptiste and his dogs a whole day to get there and another day to get back.

Last winter, for the first time, Baptiste had a wireless set. Before that, there were months and months in every year when he had no way of learning what was happening in the outside world.

You can easily imagine how much Baptiste enjoys his trip to the trading-station each spring. He hears news of the outside world from the traders, and he meets friends whom he never sees at any other time. They too are trappers, and each one wants to hear what has happened to the others during the winter.

Baptiste usually stays several days at the trading-station. With the money that the traders pay him for

Photo: Fox

In one of the trains of London's network
of Underground Railways

Photo: Alfieri

An Underground entrance when Londoners
are going home from work

his pelts he buys food and other supplies for the next winter. He buys new traps to replace old ones that have worn out, and often he buys a new gun. Always he buys presents to take home to his wife and baby.

Can you picture Baptiste as he starts back up the river on the long journey home? The canoe is loaded with things he has bought. The paddling is harder than when he came down the river, for now he is going upstream against the current. But Baptiste is happy.

He turns to take a last look at the trading-station and to wave good-bye to a friend. Then he bends to his paddle. Ahead of him stretches the winding ribbon of water that leads homeward through the quiet, lonely forest. Baptiste smiles and hums a little old French tune.

2. IN LONDON

Now let us see what is happening to another young man at the very time when Baptiste is starting to paddle home to his little cabin in the North Woods of Canada. Baptiste's watch points to 11.30 in the morning.

In London it is half-past five in the afternoon, closing time for the business offices in the City. The day has been warm for the season, and the clerks are thankful that the time for stopping work has come.

John Prior is standing by the desk where he spends five and a half days a week keeping accounts for his employer. He is putting away the last of his papers. He takes his hat and hurries to the lift. The lift is crowded, but John squeezes in, and down he goes to the ground floor of the great office building.

8

From the doors of all the banks and office buildings hundreds of clerks are streaming towards the entrance to the Underground Station. John joins them. At the station entrance he hands a penny to the newsboy and takes his evening paper. Soon he is seated in an electric train, opening his newspaper to see what has happened in the world since morning.

The train speeds through one of the long tunnels which form the great network of the Underground Railways in London. Each time the train stops, a great many people get off, but almost as many get on.

John rides to the end of the line. There he boards a crowded bus. The bus, with many a stop and start, will take him to the corner of the road where he lives. From his seat by the window he watches the

Photo: Alfieri

One of the streets in busy, crowded London

lines of passing motor-cars and the swarms of people on the pavements. He reads the cinema signs, and looks at the things displayed in the shop windows.

But John isn't really thinking about any of these sights, for he sees them every day of his life. He is thinking how good it will be to get home. He wonders what the children will have to tell him about their day at school, what his wife will give him for dinner, and whether any friends will call in the evening.

When John steps out of the bus, he takes a long breath. Only a short walk now, and he will turn into the gate of the semi-detached house where his wife and children

Photo: Keystone

London Bridge when people are on their way to work in the morning

Photo: Studio Briggs

A road lined with semi-detached houses in one of London's many suburbs

will be waiting for him. He steps along briskly, happy to be out of the pushing and crowding.

The road where the Priors live is only one of thousands in the suburbs of London. The houses stand close together with only a little space between them. There are more people living in any one of these roads than on all the land for many miles round Baptiste's cabin in the great North Woods of Canada.

This is one of the strange and interesting things about the world in which we live. Some parts of it are so crowded with people that there is scarcely room for any more.

Other parts have so few people that they are very lonely lands. There is one whole continent which has no people at all.

Would you like to know why people are not spread out more evenly over the earth? That is one of the things which we are going to learn in our study of geography in this book.

Something to do

See if you can think of any reasons why some parts of the earth have so few people while other parts are so crowded. A comparison of the two maps on the next page will suggest one reason, and perhaps you can think of others.

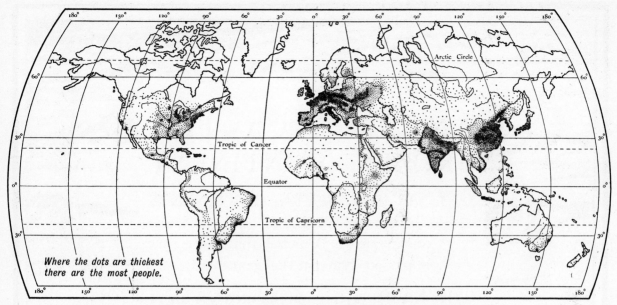

Where the dots are thickest there are the most people.

A map of the world showing distribution of population

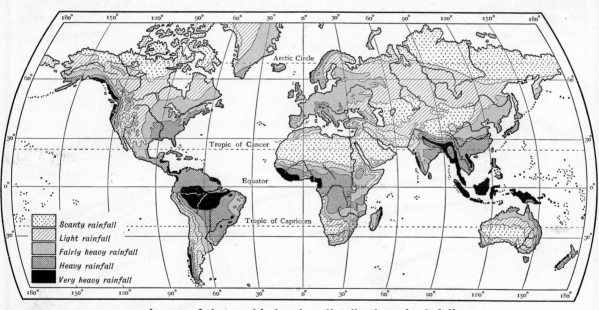

Scanty rainfall
Light rainfall
Fairly heavy rainfall
Heavy rainfall
Very heavy rainfall

A map of the world showing distribution of rainfall

You can read these maps easily if you will first study the key in the lower left corner of each one. How can you tell from the upper map where the most people live? How can you tell where the fewest people live?

How can you tell from the lower map which are the rainiest lands? How can you tell which are the driest lands? By comparing the two maps, what do you discover about the number of people in the lands of scanty rainfall?

ANTARCTICA—THE FROZEN CONTINENT

ONE OF THE SEVEN CONTINENTS of the earth is not inhabited. Do you know what this means? It means that there isn't a single person living in that continent.

THE NAME of this uninhabited continent is Antarctica. Do you know where it is situated? Can you explain why no one has ever gone there to make a permanent home, and why, probably, no one ever will?

YOU WILL FIND the answers to these questions in this chapter. As you read about Antarctica, you will be learning about the loneliest land in the whole world.

Photo: H. G. Ponting

Summer in Antarctica — penguins on the shore and an iceberg floating out to sea

CHAPTER TWO

ANTARCTICA—THE FROZEN CONTINENT

1. SOME BRAVE EXPLORERS

HAVE you ever heard of Captain Scott? He was a naval officer, and one of our bravest explorers. Explorers, you know, are people who go off to unknown and often dangerous places and bring back reports of what they discover there.

Captain Scott and four companions lost their lives on an exploring trip in Antarctica in the year 1912. One of the men died as the result of an accident. Captain Scott and the other three were frozen to death. This happened at the end of the summer season in the loneliest land in all the world.

Perhaps you can find a book which tells how these brave men fought their way over snow and ice, dragging the sledge on which they

Photo: H. G. Ponting

Captain Scott on the edge of some rough ice
on the frozen coast of Antarctica

carried their tent and their food, and how they were caught in a terrible blizzard. They struggled on in the wind and the blinding snow until they were worn out and could go no farther.

The weather was bitterly cold. The men had no shelter except their canvas tent, and their food supplies ran short. If they could have kept moving, they might have saved themselves from freezing, but they had no strength left to battle with the raging snowstorm.

Captain Scott went to Antarctica in the hope of reaching the South Pole. Perhaps you know that the South Pole is the southernmost point on the surface of the earth.

Three years earlier Rear-Admiral Peary had succeeded in reaching the North Pole, which is the northern-most point on the earth. Peary was an American naval officer. He hoisted the American flag at

the North Pole and then returned to his country. When he reached a settlement from which he could telegraph, he sent this message to the people of the United States :

"Have nailed the Stars and Stripes to the Pole ! "

Peary's message was a joking way of letting his countrymen know that he had reached the northernmost point on the earth. There is no real post or pole there. Nor is there any real post or pole at the southernmost point of the earth. "Pole" is just the name that we give to these points farthest north and farthest south.

Captain Scott hoped that he and his men would be the first explorers to reach the South Pole, and that

A map of Antarctica. The arrows show Captain
Scott's route to the South Pole

14

the Union Jack would be the first flag to be hoisted there, but in this he was disappointed. When he reached the Pole, he found that a party of Norwegian explorers, led by Captain Amundsen, had been there only a little more than a month earlier.

Like all good sportsmen, Captain Scott and his men made the best of their disappointment, and started for home. It was on the way back to the coast of Antarctica that they lost their lives.

Captain Scott and his companions died, but they did not fail. They undertook one of the most dangerous journeys in the world, and they reached their goal. If they had not met with such dreadful weather, they would have returned in safety.

Some things to do

1. Explain as clearly as you can where Captain Scott was when he hoisted the Union Jack at the South Pole.
2. Explain as clearly as you can where Rear-Admiral Peary was when he hoisted the Stars and Stripes at the North Pole.
3. Point in the direction of the North Pole, and then in the direction of the South Pole.
4. If you have a globe in your classroom, find both Poles on it.

Photo: Lieut. H. R. Bowers

Captain Scott and his men at the South Pole. The man sitting at the left pulled a string to work the camera

2. WHY ANTARCTICA IS SO COLD

You will remember we said that Captain Scott and his companions were frozen to death at the end of the summer season. Are you wondering why Antarctica is so cold even in the summer-time?

Your classroom globe (or the maps on pages 22-23 in this book) will help you to discover one of the reasons. You will find that Antarctica is the southernmost of the seven continents of the earth. The Far South, like the Far North, is cold the whole year round.

Perhaps you have thought that all the lands to the south of us are warmer than our country. That is not correct. Turn to the globe or the maps again and find the line marked "Equator". You will see

Photo ; H. G. Ponting

Captain Scott's ship in the pack-ice near the coast of Antarctica

that this line runs round the middle of the globe, halfway between the North Pole and the South Pole.

The Equator is not a real line on the earth itself. It is simply a line drawn on maps and globes to help us in finding places on the earth and in measuring distances north and south. It is the dividing line between the Northern Hemisphere and the Southern Hemisphere.

The warmest regions of the earth are found in a broad belt on both sides of the Equator. Southwards from this belt, as well as northwards, the weather gradually becomes cooler until, in the Far North and the Far South, it is very cold.

So, you see, if you travel southwards from Britain, you come first to warmer lands. But if you travel far enough south, you come again to cooler regions, and finally to the frozen land of Antarctica.

One reason, then, why Antarctica is so cold is that it is the continent of the Far South. Another reason is that Antarctica is a high land. Much of the continent is a high plateau, and in certain regions explorers have discovered high mountains. High lands, even near the Equator, are cool, and high lands far from the Equator are very cold.

Antarctica is so cold that it lies buried under a thick cap of snow and ice that never melts away. In the winter-time it has no sunshine, for the sun never once rises above the horizon. For months the days and nights are one long period of dim twilight, made a little lighter only when the moon shines brightly. This long period without any sun is called the " winter night ".

Can you imagine what it would be like to spend the long " winter night " in Antarctica? A few exploring parties have done that, but only by making the most careful preparations. They carried to Antarctica wood to build huts to live in, stoves and fuel to keep from freezing, and every bit of food that they would need for their entire stay.

The men of these exploring expeditions had to stay cooped up in their little huts during most of the long " winter night ". Often the weather was so cold that no one dared go out-of-doors for more than

Photo: H. G. Ponting

How Captain Scott's hut looked at the beginning of the summer in Antarctica

a few minutes at a time. Bitter winds swept down from the ice-cap, bringing snowstorms that almost buried the little huts. The men had to wait for the " summer day " to do most of their exploring.

Perhaps you can tell from the name what the " summer day " is in Antarctica. It is the long period in the warmer half of the year when the sun never sets. During these months the sun is never very high in the sky, but it never once disappears below the horizon. The " summer day " is one long period of daylight.

Yet even in the summer-time Antarctica is so cold that anyone who goes there must wear fur clothes like an Eskimo. No one ever does go there except explorers.

Along certain parts of the coast of Antarctica the great ice-cap extends far beyond the shore-line, forming huge shelves of thick ice over the water. In other places long tongues of thick, rough ice come down to the water's edge. These giant tongues of ice are called *glaciers*, and they move very, very slowly down to the sea.

Photo: H. G. Ponting

An Antarctic iceberg frozen into pack-ice

3. THE LONELIEST LAND

Antarctica is larger than Europe, yet not a single person lives there. Do you need to be told why? It is because there is no food to be had there.

This great continent of the Far South is much too cold for any plants or trees to grow. It is too cold for any of the farm animals that supply people with milk and meat in so many warmer lands. Even thick-furred animals like bears cannot live there because there is nothing for them to eat. Antarctica is a continent without any land animals.

In the surrounding seas there are seals and whales, and along the icy shores a few kinds of birds are found. In the summer certain kinds of gulls fly southward to Antarctica from warmer regions farther north, but the only birds that live there all the year round are the penguins.

Perhaps you remember that there are glaciers among many of the high mountains of the world, like the Alps in Switzerland. People often call glaciers "rivers of ice", but they move so slowly that they seem to be standing still.

In the summer-time huge blocks of ice break away from the outer edges of the ice-shelves in Antarctica and from the lower ends of the glaciers. These blocks form giant icebergs which float out to sea.

During the winter the waters for many, many miles round Antarctica are covered with ice so thick that no ship can break through it. In the summer this "pack-ice", as it is called, breaks up and floats away. But the summer weather is never warm enough to melt the thick cap of ice and snow that covers the land. Winter and summer, year in and year out, Antarctica is a cold, frozen continent.

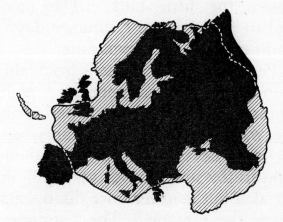

A diagram showing that Antarctica is larger than the continent of Europe

Penguins are large sea-fowl that swim but cannot fly. When they swim, they use their stubby wings as paddles. When they run, they scamper along "on all fours", but when they walk they stand upright, and from a distance they look like little old men in black coats and white waistcoats.

A few people might live for a short time along the shores of Antarctica by killing seals, whales, and penguins and eating their meat. But there is no way in which even one family could live there permanently unless food was sent to them regularly from warmer lands.

You can understand now why Antarctica is the loneliest land in the world. No one has ever gone there to make a home, and probably no one ever will.

Photo: H. G. Ponting

A mother seal and her baby on the ice

Some questions about the Far South

1. What is the South Pole?
2. In which of the seven continents is it situated?
3. Why are there no farms or pasture-lands in that continent?
4. Why couldn't Captain Scott and his men get food by hunting on their way back from the South Pole?
5. Why couldn't they build wood fires to keep from freezing?
6. What is meant by the "winter night" and the "summer day" in Antarctica?
7. Why cannot ships reach Antarctica in the winter-time?
8. Why is Antarctica so cold, even in the summer-time? You should be able to give two reasons.
9. Why are there no villages or towns there?

Some things to prove

Use the maps on pages 22-23 to prove that:

1. Antarctica is in the Southern Hemisphere.
2. The British Isles are in the Northern Hemisphere.
3. The British Isles are much nearer to the North Pole than they are to the South Pole.

THE NOMAD LANDS

DO YOU KNOW what nomads are? They are people who have no fixed homes. They are wandering people, who move about from one place to another instead of living in the same place all the time.

THE NOMAD LANDS are the parts of the earth where the different groups of nomads live their wandering lives. Can you name any of these lands?

IN THIS CHAPTER we are going to learn where the nomad lands are situated, and how the groups of wandering people make their living. Have you any idea why such people cannot have fixed homes as we have?

An explorer travelling with his dog-sledge over the ice-cap in Greenland

CHAPTER THREE

THE NOMAD LANDS

1. EXPLORING WITH GLOBES AND MAPS

NOT many of us can be explorers and go off to discover the secrets of unknown lands. But there is one way in which we can all go exploring if we wish. We can study globes and maps, and find out from them many interesting things about the world in which we live.

For example, here is a question to which you can find the answer by studying your classroom globe: Is there any large continent situated in the Far North as Antarctica is situated in the Far South?

A globe or map is a sort of record of what thousands of real explorers have discovered about the continents and oceans of the earth. The facts which you can discover from it were first learned by brave men who dared to sail out on unknown seas and make their way into unknown lands.

If you haven't a globe in your classroom, you can use the maps on pages 22-23 in this book instead.

NORTH POLE

GREENLAND

ARCTIC
OCEAN

ARCTIC CIRCLE

NORTH

AMERICA

ATLANTIC

PACIFIC

TROPIC OF CANCER

WEST

EQUATOR

170°   140°   110°   80°   50°

EAST

SOUTH

AMERICA

OCEAN

TROPIC OF CAPRICORN

OCEAN

NEW
ZEALAND

ANTARCTIC CIRCLE

ANTARCTICA

SOUTH POLE

A map of the Western Hemisphere

First find the line marked "Ant-arctic Circle", far to the south of the Equator. The part of the earth which is within the Antarctic Circle is called the *south frigid zone*, or the *south polar cap*. What continent is situated almost wholly within the south polar cap?

Now find the Arctic Circle. This line is exactly as far north of the

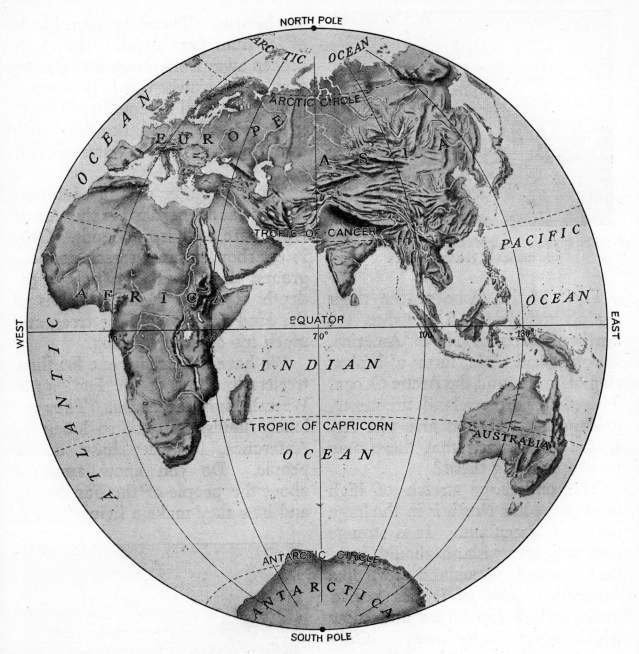

A map of the Eastern Hemisphere

Equator as the Antarctic Circle is south of the Equator. The part of the earth within the Arctic Circle is called the *north frigid zone*, or the *north polar cap*. When you have found the north polar cap, you will see that there is no large continent situated there as Antarctica is situated in the south polar cap. What ocean do you find in the north polar cap?

23

Oxford Ellesmere Land Expedition

The tupik, or tent, of an Eskimo family on
the tundra of North America

Look at the globe or the maps again, and you will see that the northern parts of North America, Europe, and Asia form a broken ring of land round the Arctic Ocean. These Far Northern lands are mostly lowlands. Does that give you any reason for thinking that there may be people living there?

The only large stretch of high land in the Far North is in the large island of Greenland. It is strange that this great island should have been named Greenland, for, like Antarctica, most of it lies buried under a thick cap of ice and snow which never melts away. Only round the shores is there any green to be seen, and even there only in the summer-time.

Perhaps you know that people travelling across the northern part of the Atlantic Ocean in the spring often see huge icebergs floating southwards. These are giant blocks of ice from Greenland. They have broken away from the ends of glaciers that creep slowly down to the sea from the coastal mountains of Greenland. Little by little they melt away in the warmer waters farther south.

For the greater part of each year the lowlands bordering the Arctic Ocean are cold, frozen lands. Only in the short summer season does the ground thaw, and then only to the depth of a few inches. Lands of this kind are too cold for trees, and much too cold for farming.

We have a special name for these treeless lowlands of the Far North. We call them the *tundra*. They are lonely lands, but not so lonely as Antarctica, for they have a few people. Do you know anything about the people of the Far North, and how they make a living there?

Photo: Hudson's Bay Co.

A giant iceberg from Greenland seen from
the deck of a ship

The men in this picture are Lapps and the animals are reindeer

2. THE FAR NORTH AND ITS WANDERING PEOPLES

THE REINDEER LANDS

THE picture on this page was taken in the summer-time in the part of Europe which we call Lapland. Lapland is not a separate country, but simply the home of the Lapps, in the northern parts of Norway, Sweden, and Finland.

Map IV at the back of this book will show you that Lapland is in the Far North of Europe, beyond the Arctic Circle. Part of it is hilly and mountainous, and the remainder is low tundra bordering the Arctic Ocean. Some of the valleys and lower mountain slopes are wooded, but the higher slopes and the tundra are too cold for trees to grow.

The Lapps live in small groups of several families each. A few of the groups live along the mountainous coast of Norway and make their living chiefly by fishing. Some others live in tiny villages in the wooded valleys, where they manage to keep a few cattle and sheep.

Most of the Lapps, however, make their living by keeping herds of reindeer, and these groups are nomads. They lead wandering lives because the reindeer cannot get sufficient food in any one place throughout the year.

The reindeer dig down through the snow to get food in the winter-time

The chief food of the reindeer is the "reindeer moss" that grows in the Far Northern lands. In the winter the animals have to dig for the moss because the ground is covered with snow. Fortunately, they have broad, sharp hoofs, and no matter how deep the snow may be, they can dig holes in it to get at the moss beneath.

The Lapps get most of the things they need and use from their herds of reindeer. They eat reindeer meat and drink reindeer milk. They use the skins to make clothing, boots, gloves, and blankets. They even make some of their tools and knives out of the horns and bones.

Each family of Lapps has a herd of fifty or more reindeer and several dogs rather like collies. Most of the reindeer are half-wild, and this makes it difficult to keep them together. The dogs help in this work as sheep dogs help shepherds in our country.

Besides the main herd, every Lapp family has a number of reindeer which are trained to draw sledges over the snow. The Lapps use the sledges chiefly for carrying their belongings when they are travelling. The men travel on skis. So do many of the women and children. Usually, only the old people, the mothers who have babies, and the little children ride on the sledges.

The last sledge in a Lapp procession carries the tent-poles and coverings. When the Lapps reach a place where they wish to camp, the men of each family set up their tent-poles in a circle, slanting them so that they all meet at the top. When the cloth covering has been wrapped round the poles, each family has a snug little cone-shaped house. In the middle of it a fire is built, and round the fire are spread deer-skins for beds and blankets.

Photo: Stig Wesslen

This little Lapp girl is going for a sledge-ride and the boy for a run on his skis

Each group of Lapp families has a special place where they spend the winter. Usually it is in a wooded valley, where there is shelter from the cold winds and where firewood is easily obtained. Always it must be where reindeer moss is plentiful. For winter houses some of the Lapps have little round huts built of wood or stones and covered with sods to make them warmer. Others live in their tents both in winter and in summer.

Map IV at the back of the book shows that the tundra stretches eastwards from Lapland across the northern part of Russia and Siberia to the Pacific Ocean. Scattered here and there over this great stretch of Arctic lowlands are other groups of reindeer-herders who live in much the same way as the Lapps.

Winter in the Far North is long and very cold. The frozen tundra is covered with snow, and icy winds sweep over it from the Arctic Ocean. At many places along the coast it is hard to see where the land ends and the water begins, because of the thick pack-ice which forms on the water.

Like the Far South, the Far North has a period of "winter night". For many weeks the sun does not rise. During this period the days are dark and gloomy as well as bitterly cold.

South of the tundra in Russia and Siberia, there are forests. There, in scattered spots along the northern edge of the forests, the small groups of reindeer-herders spend the winter. Like some of the Lapps, they live in huts built of wood and sods.

27

Photo: Buffalo Museum

A picture of a model showing the summer tent and the winter hut of a Lapp family

Spring is late in coming to the Far North, but when it does come, it comes quickly. The snow melts away, and soon the mossy tundra is covered with patches of coarse grass and with small plants which have bright-coloured flowers.

The summer is short, but it is warmer than you might expect because for a good part of it the sun shines night and day. While it lasts, the tundra, dotted with the gay blossoms of wild flowers, is a lovely sight. But in spite of its beauty, the tundra is not a pleasant place where anyone would care to spend a summer holiday. The ground is so soft and boggy that in many parts walking is difficult. Worse than that, there are swarms of gnats, mosquitoes, and other insects that sting and bite.

When spring comes, the reindeer-herders of Russia and Siberia begin to move northwards towards the Arctic Ocean. As long as there is any snow on the ground they use their sledges and skis. After that, the sledge-animals are used as pack-animals, carrying the few belongings of each family on their backs. Skis must be given up now, and the people must walk.

The reindeer walk over the boggy tundra more easily than the people because their hoofs are so broad. Their broad hoofs also keep them from sinking deeply into the snow in winter.

Meanwhile, the Lapps farther west are also starting on their summer wanderings. They too are on their way from their winter quarters to grazing-grounds nearer the sea.

28

These nomads of the Far North do not drive their herds of half-wild reindeer as our shepherds drive flocks of sheep. The reindeer take the lead, and the people follow. The men and dogs simply keep the herds from breaking up and scattering.

The people pitch their tents wherever the reindeer stop to graze for some time. There they stay until the animals have eaten most of the moss in the neighbourhood. When the reindeer start for another feeding-place, the people take down their tents and follow the herd.

The summer wanderings carry many of the reindeer-herders to the shores of the Arctic Ocean. There the men often do a little fishing. Fish is a pleasant change from the reindeer meat which the people live on for most of the year.

Summer comes to an end rather suddenly in the Far North, and with the first fall of snow the return trip begins. Before the snow covers the ground very deeply, the reindeer and their owners are back at their winter quarters.

Winter in the wooded valleys of Lapland and on the edge of the forest in Russia and Siberia is not so unpleasant as you might think. The weather, of course, is bitterly cold, but the nomads do not mind it. They keep snug and warm in their little huts because they can

Photo : D. Carruthers

A group of Siberian reindeer-herders who live in much the same way as the Lapps

get plenty of firewood. They have warm fur clothing, and with their reindeer grazing close by, there is always meat for food.

During the winter some of the men do a little hunting or fur-trapping in the woods. Often they go off on long ski-ing trips just for the fun of it. They have plenty of spare time because the reindeer look after themselves. The reindeer find their own food, and they do not even have to be given water to drink, for they eat snow instead.

During the winter the men often make trips to the nearest settlements where traders have shops. They load their sledges with deerskins and meat which they can spare, and in the settlements they exchange these products of their herds for flour, coffee, and such things as knives, guns, and cloth.

29

CHAPTER THREE

Photo: Dorien Leigh

Some Lapp children and the huts in which they live while at school in the winter

THE ESKIMOS
OF THE AMERICAN TUNDRA

The people of the tundra of North America are mostly Eskimos. For a long, long time all the Eskimos made their living by hunting and fishing. For some reason they did not tame the wild reindeer as the people of the tundra of Europe and Asia did, and so they did not become reindeer-herders.

Turn to Map I at the front of this book and find Alaska, the north-western part of North America. Alaska belongs to the United States of America. Except for Greenland, the remainder of the Far Northern lands of the Western Hemisphere are part of the Dominion of Canada. Greenland belongs to Denmark, one of the countries which are near neighbours of ours in the continent of Europe.

About fifty years ago the government of the United States had some herds of reindeer sent over to Alaska from Siberia. The men who brought the reindeer to Alaska were Lapps and Siberians, and they taught the Eskimos how to become reindeer-herders. There were only a few hundred reindeer in Alaska at first, but now there are hundreds of thousands. Most of the Alaskan Eskimos now make their living by keeping herds of these useful animals instead of by hunting and fishing.

Perhaps you wonder what the children do in the winter-time. They spend a good deal of time out-of-doors on their skis, or playing with the dogs in the snow. In some parts of the Far North the nomad children are sent to school for a few months each winter in villages to the south. But they always return to their families before it is time to start on the summer wanderings.

Some things to do

1. Pretend that you are a Lapp boy or girl. Explain how you and your family manage to make a living in the cold lands of the Far North.

2. Explain why no one can make a living in that way in Antarctica, in the Far South.

3. See if you can make a model of a Lapp camp like the one in the picture on page 28. Perhaps some other children will like to help you.

Photo: Canadian Official News Bureau

A snapshot of a few of the Canadian government's herd of reindeer taken during
the long " drive " across the frozen tundra from Alaska

A few years ago the Canadian government decided to help some of the Eskimos in Canada to become reindeer-herders. A large herd of reindeer was purchased in Alaska. With three Lapps in charge, the animals were driven eastwards to the part of the tundra which lies east of the Mackenzie River.

You would enjoy reading about this great reindeer drive, for it took five years, and the herders had many adventures. It was very hard to keep the herd together and to prevent the animals from turning back, for reindeer, as you know, are not easily driven like sheep.

Much of the North American tundra is just as good pasture-land for reindeer as the tundra of Europe and Asia, and in time perhaps more of the Eskimos will become reindeer-herders. At present, however, reindeer-herding is carried on only in Alaska and one small section of the Canadian tundra. Elsewhere the Eskimos still make their living by hunting and fishing.

Like the reindeer-herders, the Eskimo hunters live wandering lives, but for a different reason. They wander in search of the wild animals which they kill for food and clothing materials. They hunt the walrus, seals, and narwhal (sea-unicorn) that live in the Far Northern seas, and the caribou (wild reindeer) and other animals that live on the land. Sometimes they kill a whale or a huge polar bear.

Photos: Oxford Ellesmere Land Expedition

Eskimo hunters landing a narwhal they have killed

A good catch of fish

The meat and the blubber, or fat, of the wild animals provide the Eskimo hunting tribes with most of their food. The blubber also supplies the oil which the Eskimos burn for heat and light.

The fur-covered skins of the animals supply the warm clothing that the Eskimos need, and are useful in many other ways. Deerskins make warm blankets. Sealskins, sewed together, make the tupiks, or tents, in which the Eskimos live in the summer-time. Strips of walrus-hide make good harness for the dogs which the Eskimos use to draw their sledges over the snow in the winter-time.

All the Eskimos do a little fishing; some of them a good deal. Certain groups catch large numbers of salmon in the summer. They dry the salmon to keep it from spoiling, and store it away for the winter.

The Eskimos live in small groups of a few families each. In the summer they often wander hundreds of miles on their hunting-trips. They travel along the shores in their boats, and they camp wherever they find good seal-hunting or good walrus-hunting. They eat what they need of the meat and blubber of the animals they kill. The rest they store away for the winter.

Sometime during the summer most of the Eskimo groups go inland to places where the caribou feed on the moss and grass. Caribou-hunting is part of their summer work, for they need the skins for blankets and clothing, and the meat to add to their food-supply for the winter.

The families of each group of Eskimo hunters have a special place where they spend the long, cold winters. They do not go into the woods as the reindeer-herders do.

Their winter quarters are along the shores of the frozen seas. That is because they have no herds of animals to provide them with food. For their winter homes they choose spots where they can get food by hunting seals and by fishing through holes in the ice.

Perhaps you remember that the Eskimos call their little round winter houses "igloos". Many of the groups live in igloos built of stones and covered with sods. Other groups live in igloos built of blocks of hard-packed snow.

The better luck the Eskimos have in hunting in the summer, the better prepared they are with food for the winter. But even with the best of luck, they cannot get enough meat and blubber in the summer to last the long winter through. So, in spite of the cold, the Eskimo men go hunting in the winter whenever the weather is not too stormy.

You can easily see that the life of the Eskimo hunters is harder than the life of the reindeer-herders. The herders have only to wander with their animals to be sure of having food. The hunters are never quite sure when or where they will find the wild animals on which their food-supply depends.

Yet the Eskimos are among the most cheerful, happy people in the world. The families in each group

By courtesy of Révillion Frères

This Eskimo father has brought home a good "catch" of deerskins on his back

share their food-supplies with one another. At times there may not be very much food for anyone, but no one is allowed to go hungry when others have more than they barely need to eat. The Eskimos take good luck and bad luck as it comes, and keep smiling through it all.

Do you know

1. Why the Eskimo hunting tribes cannot live in one place all the time?
2. At what time of year they lead wandering lives, and why?
3. Why they choose places along the shores of the northern seas for their winter homes?
4. Why their life is harder than the life of the reindeer-herders?

Something to think about

If you belonged to an Eskimo hunting tribe, would you like your government to give you a herd of reindeer? Give reasons for your answer.

Four important animals of the Far North. Can you name each one and explain its usefulness to the Far Northern peoples?

WHY THE FAR NORTH HAS SO FEW PEOPLE

If you will look at the upper map on page 11, you will see that the lands of the Far North have very few people. The small groups of hunters and reindeer-herders are scattered far and wide over huge, lonely stretches of land, which are cold and frozen most of the year. Can you explain why there are not more people in these great stretches of land?

It is because the Far North is so cold. The summer is too short and too cool for the growth of plants which provide food in warmer lands. In all but a very few places the weather is too cold for animals such as cattle, pigs, or even sheep. Even if these animals could live through the winter cold, they would die of starvation, for there would be no way of feeding them.

Only in lands where food is plentiful can large numbers of people make their homes. Either the people must be able to grow crops and keep farm animals that supply food, or they must have ways of getting plenty of food from outside.

In the Far North the people cannot grow crops for food. The only animals they can keep for food are reindeer. Furthermore, these cold lands are so far from the farming regions of the world that the people cannot get much food from outside.

Perhaps you wonder why more people cannot live in the Far North by keeping reindeer. There are two reasons. One reason is that it takes a herd of at least fifty reindeer to keep a family of five people supplied with food throughout the year. The other reason is that each herd of reindeer needs a very large area of land over which to wander in order to get enough moss to keep alive and healthy. So, you see, the reindeer lands can never support a very large number of people.

It is much the same with the hunting-grounds. If many more people tried to make their living by hunting in the Far North, food-supplies for all would soon be scarce. The wild animals would be killed off so fast that in time there would be none left.

You can understand now why the cold regions of the Far North are lonely lands, and why they will probably never have many more people than they have to-day.

A family of nomads in the steppes of Asia

Photo: D. Carruthers

Some questions about the Far North

1. What is the North Pole? In the midst of which ocean is it situated?

2. What do we call the treeless plains that border that ocean?

3. In which three continents are these plains of the Far North?

4. What large island in the Far North has a thick cap of ice and snow much like Antarctica?

5. That island is sometimes called the "birthplace of icebergs". Can you explain why?

6. Why are there no forests on the tundra? Why are there no farms?

7. Why can't these Arctic plains be used as pasture-lands for cattle and sheep? What do reindeer find to eat there?

8. Why are the reindeer-herders and the hunters of the Far North nomads?

9. Why do we call the Far Northern lands "lonely lands"?

10. What reasons have you to think that these lands will never be crowded with people?

3. THE STEPPES AND DESERTS

THE WANDERING KIRGHIZ

Here is a picture of a family of Kirghiz people. The Kirghiz are nomads, and they live in the part of Asia which is called the Kirghiz Steppe.

Behind the people in the picture is their tent, or *yurt*, as it is called. It is made of a light lattice framework of wood which can be folded up and carried on the back of an animal whenever the people move. In winter the yurt is covered with felt for warmth and protection against the wind. In summer it is screened with matting of woven reeds.

The Kirghiz make their living by rearing sheep, goats, cattle, and horses. They use horses for riding, and oxen for carrying their belongings when they move. Their food is mainly mutton from the sheep,

Photo: D. Carruthers

Putting up the lattice framework of a yurt

Photo: Dorien Leigh

The felt covering makes a yurt wind-proof

milk from the cows, sheep, goats, and mares, and cheese made from the milk. The Kirghiz are especially fond of koumiss, a sour drink which is prepared from mares' milk. It tastes rather like buttermilk.

The word "steppe" means a region which has too little rain for trees, but enough for the growth of short grass. The steppes, then, are rather dry lands. For the most part they are too dry for farming, but they make fairly good pasture-lands.

The Kirghiz steppe is a lowland plain, with a covering of rather thin grass. It is a large region, situated in a part of Asia where the winters are cold and the summers hot. In the winter-time the ground freezes, and it is sometimes covered with a light fall of snow. During that season the people are chilly in their yurts, for bitterly cold winds sweep over the steppe.

When spring comes and the ground thaws, new green grass springs up quickly. Soon, however, the grass withers in the hot summer sun, and becomes brown and dry. Dry, withered grass makes poorer pasturage for animals than fresh, green grass.

Here and there in the Kirghiz Steppe there are hills, and on its eastern margin there are mountains. These higher lands get more snow in winter and more rain in summer than the steppe itself. More rain in summer means thicker and greener grass, so the higher lands are the better summer pastures.

You can easily understand why the Kirghiz are nomadic people. Since they depend on their flocks and herds for most of their food and other needs, they must drive their animals to the places where the best grass is to be found at different times of year.

In winter the Kirghiz live in encampments on the steppe. These encampments are clusters of yurts in the midst of the winter grazing-lands. They are always in places where drinking-water for the people and the animals can be obtained from a stream, or from springs or wells.

The spots chosen for winter quarters by the nomads are sometimes close to tiny settlements where a few people have fixed homes. The people of these villages are not Kirghiz. They are farming folk who have settled in the valley of some stream from which they can get water for the growing of a few crops in the summer-time. Their settlements are few and far between, because streams are not plentiful in the steppe.

During the winter the cattle, sheep, and goats of the Kirghiz often have to paw through the snow to get grass to eat. Fortunately, the snow is seldom very deep, but the winter grass is poor, and by spring the animals often become very thin. The horses fare a little better, for their masters usually buy winter feed for them from the farmers.

In spring, with new green grass to eat, the animals soon begin to put on more flesh. Then comes the time when they leave the steppe for the higher pastures among the hills and mountains.

Three guests in a Kirghiz yurt. They are being given koumiss in wooden bowls

There are two reasons why the Kirghiz take their flocks and herds to the higher lands for the summer. One is that the grass is thicker and greener there. The other reason is that if the animals grazed on the steppe all the summer, they would eat so much of the grass that there would be little left for them to feed on in the winter.

You would be interested to see a group of Kirghiz families on the march. The men ride ahead on their small, swift horses. The main procession is made up of the cattle, sheep, and goats, driven by the older boys and girls. Bringing up the rear are the women. They ride on horses or oxen, and they take charge of all the pack-animals which carry the yurts and other luggage strapped on their backs. The little children ride with their mothers, or on ponies of their own.

Photo: Akademia

The first snow has fallen, and the nomads are on the way to their winter quarters

It often takes the Kirghiz several days to reach their summer quarters, for there are steep slopes to climb. Then, too, the cattle, sheep, and goats walk slowly, stopping to feed here and there as they go. At midday the whole company stops for a short rest. Every evening the luggage is unloaded, the yurts set up, and the animals milked and tethered for the night.

Most of the Kirghiz live in groups of a few families each. None of the groups owns any land, but each one has grazing rights in a certain part of the steppe and the neighbouring hills or mountains. That means that the government under which the Kirghiz live grants to the people of each group certain lands where they, and they alone, may pasture their animals.

The journeys to and fro between the summer and winter pastures are often long and hard. In the spring the nomads sometimes have to cross dangerously swift streams, swollen with water from the melting snow on the higher lands. In the autumn, on their way down from the hills and mountains, they are sometimes caught in blinding snowstorms.

During the months when the Kirghiz are settled in their winter quarters or their summer quarters, their life is not so hard. The men and boys watch over the flocks and herds in the pastures, now and then riding off to find an animal that has strayed away. Whenever skins are needed for leather, or meat is needed for food, they kill a few of their sheep or cattle, and in the spring they shear the sheep for their wool.

The women do the daily work of milking, making cheese and koumiss, and preparing meals. In addition to these tasks, they make much of the clothing for themselves and their families.

From sheepskins with the wool left on, the women make the heavy coats and big caps which their men-folk wear. From the sheep's wool, they weave rugs for furnishings for the yurts, and cloth for clothing and blankets. They also make the felt for the yurt coverings. They do this by beating wool and goats' hair until it sticks together firmly and forms thick, waterproof cloth.

The things which the Kirghiz need, but cannot make themselves, they buy mostly from travelling pedlars. The pedlars go from one camp to another with supplies such as tea, flour, cotton cloth, guns, and knives. They take in exchange the wool, hides, and skins which the Kirghiz have to sell.

The more animals a Kirghiz can rear, the richer he is. You can easily understand why. It is because the animals and their wool, hides, and skins are really his money, and the more he has of them, the more things he can buy from the pedlars. Those who are richest like to buy striped silk coats, fine knee-boots, and saddles and bridles trimmed with silver.

Photo: A. L. Strong

The nomad women do the milking

Not many of the Kirghiz, however, are rich, and even the richest ones never know when the weather may make them poor. If the winter is unusually cold, many of their animals are sure to die. If the summer is unusually dry, and there is less grass and water than are needed, hunger and thirst may cause many deaths among the animals.

The loss of a large number of animals is the worst thing that can happen to a Kirghiz family. It leaves them short of food and of materials for clothing, tents, and blankets. The sale of the skins of the dead animals helps only a little. Until the flocks and herds can be

39

Photo : Lubinski

A Kirghiz horseman on the lonely steppe

built up again, the family will be poorly fed and poorly clothed.

If you were to visit the Kirghiz Steppe, you might travel for miles and miles without seeing any of the groups of wandering people. After meeting one group, you would probably travel a long distance before coming across another. This dry grassland is one of the lonely lands of the earth.

Do you remember why there are not more reindeer-herders in the tundra of the Far North? The reason why there are not more nomads on the Kirghiz Steppe is much the same.

It takes a large number of animals to supply each Kirghiz family with food, clothing, and extra wool and skins which can be sold. Each animal needs so much grass that every group of Kirghiz families must have large stretches of winter and summer pasture-land.

You can see, then, that the number of people who can live on the steppe really depends on the amount of grass. Since the animals kept by each family need a large stretch of pasture-land, the people can live only in widely-scattered groups.

Some things to explain

1. Why are there no woods or forests on the Kirghiz Steppe?
2. Why is the grass that grows there poorer than the grass that grows in the British Isles?
3. How do most of the people of the Kirghiz Steppe make their living?
4. Who among the Kirghiz are considered the richest, and why?
5. In what kind of houses do the Kirghiz live, and why?
6. Why can't their flocks and herds graze in the same pastures all the year round?
7. Why do the Kirghiz live in such widely-scattered groups?

THE GREATEST STRETCH OF DRY LANDS

If you will look at Map IV at the back of the book, you will see that the Kirghiz Steppe is only one part of the greatest stretch of dry lands in the world. Notice that these lands begin in the west with the great Sahara Desert of northern Africa, and that from there they extend north-eastwards across Arabia and central Asia.

By courtesy of John A. Boardman

This picture was taken in the northern part of the great Sahara Desert

Among these dry lands, besides those we have named, are the plateau of Iran, the Tarim Basin, and the desert which is called the Gobi. You can see for yourself how little rain these lands have by studying the lower map on page 11.

Map II at the front of the book will show you that some of these dry lands are lowland plains like the Kirghiz Steppe. Others are plateaus with high mountains along their borders. Some are warm the whole year round, while others are hot in summer but cold in winter.

In one way, however, these lands are all much alike. Not one of them has enough rain for farming, and for that reason crops can be grown only where water can be obtained from streams, springs, or wells. All these lands are either deserts or poorly-watered steppes.

Deserts, you know, are the very driest lands. There are parts of the Sahara and the Gobi where not a drop of rain falls for years at a time. For miles and miles there is nothing to be seen but bare rocky ground, or stretches of sand-dunes which have been piled up by the wind.

In many parts of the deserts, however, a little rain falls at one time or another during the year. After the rains, grass springs up in thin patches here and there. Because of the grass, small groups of nomads can live in the deserts by keeping camels, sheep, and goats.

Perhaps you remember what you learned two or three years ago about the tribes of Bedouins who live in the deserts of Arabia. There are Bedouins in the Sahara Desert too. They get most of their food and clothing materials from their flocks and herds, and they wander over the desert lands year in and year out in search of grass and water to keep their animals alive.

A 6

Photo : Raswan

A Bedouin camp in the desert of Arabia

In the deserts the camel is the nomad's best friend. It carries his belongings on its back, and makes a good riding-animal. It gives him milk to drink and hair for making tent-cloth and clothing. It can go without drinking-water for several days, and the hump of fat on its back nourishes it when no grass is to be found. When the sheep and goats are weak from hunger or thirst, the camel can still keep going.

In the steppes, the horse takes the place of the camel as a riding-animal and often serves also as a pack-animal. That is because, even in the poorer steppes, there is more rain and therefore better grass than in the deserts. In the deserts, only the richer sheiks, or nomad chiefs, can afford to keep horses.

We have taken the Kirghiz as an example of the wandering peoples of the steppes. There are other groups of nomads in the steppes of Asia who live in much the same way. The deserts have even fewer people than the steppes because they are drier and have less grass. The steppes and deserts alike are lonely lands because they are lands of scanty rainfall.

Something to do

On the lower map on page 11 find the great stretch of dry lands about which you have just read. Then look at the upper map on the same page and notice how few people live in most parts of these dry lands.

We say that lands which have so few people as this are thinly populated. What, then, is a thickly populated land?

Some questions to answer

1. Are the British Isles thinly populated, or thickly populated?
2. How can you use the upper map on page 11 to prove that your answer to question 1 is correct?

THE OASES AND THEIR PEOPLE

Here and there in the deserts of Asia and northern Africa, there are oases. If you were flying over these deserts in an aeroplane, the oases would appear as tiny spots of green separated from one another by miles and miles of bare, rocky ground and brownish sand.

The oases are green because they are places where there is enough water for the growth of trees and crops of grain, fruit, and vegetables. In most of the oases the water comes from springs and wells. That means, of course, that it is water from beneath the ground.

In some of the oases, however, the water comes

By courtesy of John A. Boardman

A camel caravan coming into a good-sized oasis town

from streams which rise in the bordering mountains and flow down the slopes to the deserts. The oases of this kind are usually near the mountains. That is because most of the streams do not get far after they reach the deserts. Either they dry up, or their waters sink into the sandy ground.

There is one very long, narrow oasis in northern Africa which is watered by the River Nile. The Nile rises in a rainy part of Africa, far to the south of the Sahara. It is so well supplied with water from its sources that it flows northwards for hundreds of miles across the almost rainless desert to the Mediterranean Sea.

All along its course through the desert, the Nile provides water for farming. The farms are on the narrow strips of lowland bordering the river, and the water needed for the crops is carried from the river to the fields through canals and ditches.

Towns and villages are strung along the Nile in Egypt and the Sudan like scattered beads on a chain. All the land between them which can be supplied with water from the river is used for growing grain, cotton, and vegetables. Perhaps you know that much cotton from the Nile oasis comes to Britain for our cotton-mills.

Find the Nile oasis on the upper map on page 11, and you will see that it is crowded with people. The Nile Valley is a thickly populated strip of farming land in the midst of a vast, thinly populated desert.

All the other oases are very much smaller. In some of them there is only water enough to support a small village. In others there is water enough to support a good-

43

A corner of the market-place in an oasis town

Photo : Dorien Leigh

For their own use the people of the oases grow grain and vegetables. The grain provides them with flour and meal for making bread, and with food for the donkeys and other animals which they keep to help them in their work.

Every grove of fruit trees and every field of grain or vegetables in an oasis must be irrigated. Perhaps that is a new word to you. It means that water must be carried to gardens, fields, and groves by means of ditches dug in the ground.

Some of the water comes from streams or springs, but more of it is taken from wells. Hundreds of donkeys, bullocks, and camels work

sized town. The number of people who can live in any oasis depends on the amount of water which can be obtained for drinking, growing crops, and other needs of the people.

The villages and towns of the small oases are clusters of mud-brick houses and tiny shops, surrounded by fields, gardens, and groves of fruit trees. The streets are narrow, and people, donkeys, and camels jostle one another as they pass to and fro. Some of these oases can be reached by motor-car, but the only way of getting to many of them is by camel caravan.

In the oases of the warm deserts date-palms are the commonest trees. The people grow the date-palms in groves, and tend them with the greatest care. In the oases of Arabia and northern Africa (with the exception of the Nile Valley) dates are almost the only product which the people send to far-away lands.

A grove of date-palms in an Arabian oasis

patiently in the oases, turning big wooden wheels that lift water from wells which the people have dug in the ground.

The oases, you see, are garden-like spots in the midst of the vast, lonely stretches of desert. Each and every one of them is crowded with as many people as can possibly live there. If, little by little, the springs and wells in an oasis dry up, the people have to move away. In many of the deserts there are places where this has happened. Towns where hundreds of people once had homes now lie in ruins, treeless, and nearly buried in drifting sand.

Photo: Dorien Leigh

Turning a well-wheel. Why is this work so important in the oases?

Some questions about oases

1. On what does the number of people who can live in an oasis depend, and why?

2. What do we mean when we say that the fields, gardens, and fruit groves in the oases are irrigated?

3. In what ways is water for irrigation obtained?

4. Why can so many people live in the valley of the River Nile?

Some questions about the nomad lands

1. In which two continents are the greatest stretches of dry lands?

2. Why are these lands warmer in summer than the tundra?

3. Why are the herdsmen of the tundra and the dry lands nomads?

4. What do we mean when we say that their lives depend on finding pasturage for their flocks and herds?

5. Why must the hunters of the tundra lead wandering lives?

6. Do you think the nomad lands will ever have a great many more people than they have now? Give reasons for your answer.

Just suppose

1. Suppose you had to choose between being a Lapp or a Kirghiz. Which would your choice be, and why?

2. Suppose a Lapp boy were to visit a Kirghiz family. What things would remind him of home? What differences would he find between the life of the Kirghiz and the life of his own people? What reasons for these differences would he discover?

LANDS OF SCATTERED SETTLEMENTS

IN THIS CHAPTER we are going to learn about the lands where people live in scattered settlements. Settlements are places where people have fixed homes.

SOME OF THESE LANDS are fairly well populated because the settlements are not far apart. Others are lonely lands because the settlements are few and far between.

OUR STUDY will take us to high lands and low lands; to dry lands and rainy lands; to warm lands and cold lands. Where in these different kinds of lands do you think we shall find the most people?

These Australian black-fellows are spearing fish, and this one has been kangaroo-hunting

CHAPTER FOUR

LANDS OF SCATTERED SETTLEMENTS

1. MORE ABOUT THE DRY LANDS

MAPS III and IV at the back of the book show that, while the greatest stretch of dry lands is in northern Africa and Asia, there are deserts and poorly-watered steppes in other parts of the world. Notice that there are lands of this kind in Australia and in North America and South America.

You know, of course, that Australia is part of the British Empire, and that most of its people are of British descent. The remainder are dark-skinned aborigines. That means that they are descended from the native people who were the only inhabitants of Australia before the white men came. In the Americas the aborigines are Red Indians.

The dry lands of Australia and the Americas are not nomad lands as the dry lands of northern Africa and Asia are. The reason for this is that the aborigines never learned to keep any domestic animals except dogs.

The Australian aborigines are called " black-fellows ", though their skin is chocolate-brown, not black. There are only a few of them left now, and they live in very small and very widely-scattered groups.

Red Indian homes in a desert region in the
south-western part of North America

The dry lands of Australia are
hot in summer and never very cold
in winter, so the black-fellows have
little need of clothing or shelter.
For the most part their houses are
nothing more than screens of rough
branches for shelter from the wind.
For food the black-fellows hunt wild
animals and birds, and collect the
seeds, berries, and roots of certain
wild plants. Those who live near
streams or the sea do a little fishing.

The Red Indians who still live
in certain parts of the dry lands of
the Americas are mostly farmers.
They live in villages which are little
clusters of houses built of mud-brick
or of stone and plaster. Their
villages are always in places where
water from streams can be used to
irrigate their fields of maize and
their vegetable gardens.

For the most part these dry lands
of Australia and the Americas are
lonely lands because of the scarcity
of water. In some places, however,
white people have made settlements
for special reasons.

In certain parts of the dry lands
in the western half of the United
States of America there are many
miles of farm-lands where once
nothing but the poorest grass and
the coarsest shrubs grew. The Americans call these farm-lands " garden
spots in the desert ". They are
lands which are irrigated with water
from reservoirs in the mountains,
many miles away. The reservoirs
are made by damming streams, and
the water is carried to the farm-
lands through very long pipe-lines or
canals.

The picture on the next page
shows a potato field in one of these
" garden spots ". You can see the
shallow channels for irrigation water
between the long rows of plants.

Photo : Dorien Leigh

One of the great reservoirs of irrigation water
in the United States of America

On these irrigated lands fine crops of grain, fruit, and vegetables are grown, and much hay and alfalfa for cattle and sheep. They are thickly populated lands with many towns, but they are widely separated from one another. Between them lie great stretches of dry land which cannot be irrigated and are useless. Like the oases of the nomad lands, these irrigated lands of America are crowded areas in the midst of miles and miles of lonely lands.

There is another reason why settlements have grown up in some of the very dry parts of Australia and the Americas. It is because in certain places there are valuable metal ores beneath the surface of the ground. You probably know that ore is rock material in which there are bits of metal such as copper, silver, or gold.

For example, in the western part of the great desert of Australia there are rich ores of gold. In order to get the gold, deep mines have been opened. Many men, of course, are needed to work in the mines, and so settlements have grown up round about them.

On the map on pages 124-125 find Kalgoorlie, in Western Australia. This is the largest of the gold-mining towns in that part of the country, and it has several thousand people. Many of them work for the mining companies. Many others work in

By courtesy of U.S.D.A.

A " garden spot " in a dry part of America

the shops and business offices which Kalgoorlie, like any other town, must have to serve the needs of its people.

Kalgoorlie is so dry that every drop of water which the people use comes from near the west coast of Australia through a huge pipe-line four hundred miles long. Nearly all their food, too, comes from outside the desert, and is brought to Kalgoorlie by railway train.

There would be no settlements in this very dry part of Western Australia if it were not for the gold which is found there. The towns have grown up because the gold is something that people in the outside world need and want.

The same thing has happened in the dry south-western parts of the United States of America, in the dry lands of Mexico, and along the desert coast of Chile in South America. In those parts of the world mining

By courtesy of Australian National Travel Association
Here are some of the gold mines at Kalgoorlie

has led to the growth of scattered settlements in places where it would be very hard for people to make a living in any other way.

When you think of the deserts and the poorer steppes of the world, remember that it is lack of water that makes them lonely lands. Remember, too, that the only places in the dry lands where many people live crowded together are the oases and other irrigated areas where farming is possible, and the scattered spots where mining is carried on.

Can you explain

1. Why a large part of Australia is very thinly populated?

2. How the Americans have made "garden spots" in some parts of their dry lands?

3. Why settlements have grown up in certain places in the deserts where there is little or no water for irrigation?

4. Why settlements in dry lands are widely scattered?

2. THE NORTHERN FORESTS
LANDS TOO COOL FOR FARMING

If you were a Canadian boy or girl, you might spend your summer holidays camping in the great North Woods. There are many things you could do to enjoy yourself there. You could fish and swim in the lakes and streams. You could go on canoe trips, and you could play at being Red Indians or explorers in the woods.

On such a holiday you would see only a tiny bit of the great forest that stretches across the northern part of North America. You would see enough of it, though, to know that this great forest is a lonely wilderness of trees and streams. To the north of it is the cold, treeless tundra, where the Eskimos live. To the south are lands where the weather is warm enough for people to make a living by farming.

In the northern part of Eurasia there is an even greater forest of the same kind. Perhaps Eurasia is a new name to you, but if you think for a moment you will not need to be told that it means Europe and Asia. These two continents are not separated from each other by any large bodies of water.

The northern forest of Eurasia extends all the way from the Scandinavian Peninsula on the west to the coast of Siberia on the east.

The reindeer-herders, you know, spend the winter on the northern margin of this great forest.

Before you read any further, find the northern forests of America and Eurasia on Maps III and IV at the back of the book. Then look at the upper map on page 11, and you will see that these great forests are very thinly populated.

How you might spend a holiday in the North Woods of Canada

The northern forests, then, are among the lonely lands of the earth. The people live in small towns and villages along the streams, or in lonely cabins in the woods. Many of the towns and villages are separated from their nearest neighbours by miles of woodland through which no roads or railways have ever been built.

The principal reason why the northern forests have few people is that they are not good lands for farming. That is not because of the trees, for the trees could be cut down if people wished to use the land for growing crops.

The trouble with the northern forests is that they have long, cold winters, and short, cool summers. That is because they are so far from the Equator. Frosty weather lasts until late in the spring, and comes again early in the autumn. For that reason there is not a long enough period of warm weather for most kinds of crops to ripen.

So, you see, it is useless to try to do very much farming in the northern forests. Most of the people of these regions must make their living in other ways. Have you any idea how they do it?

Some questions to answer

1. Where would you go in the British Empire to see one of the great northern forests?

2. Which ocean would you cross to get there?

3. Where could you see a forest of the same kind nearer home?

4. How are the northern forests different from the tundra?

5. Why are they too cool for much farming?

| Fox | Beaver | Muskrat | Lynx | Wolf | Ermine |

Here are a few of the kinds of wild animals that supply us with furs. Can you name others?

FUR-TRAPPERS AND THEIR WORK

If you remember what you read about Baptiste at the beginning of this book, you know of one way in which some of the people of the northern forests make a living. They trap the wild animals and sell the fur-covered skins.

A list of all the different animals that live in the northern forests would be very long. In it you would find several kinds of foxes; many little animals like ermines, minks, and martens; big animals such as deer and bears; water-loving animals such as otters, muskrats, and beavers; and dangerous animals such as lynxes and wolves. The fur of these animals grows very thick in the winter to keep them warm, and thins out in the summer.

It takes the pelts of millions of animals to supply all the furs worn by people in countries like ours. For fur garments the thick coats of the animals are wanted, and so trapping is done in the winter-time.

If you are reading this chapter at any time between the first of November and the first of April, you may be sure that at this very moment hundreds of trappers are trudging over lonely trails in the northern forests. Some are on snowshoes, and some on skis. Many have dog-sledges, but some are pulling their sledges themselves. Many are alone; others are working in pairs as partners. Let us see what Baptiste is doing.

Baptiste has just started out to go the rounds of his trap-line. A trap-line is the route along which, at widely-separated spots, a trapper sets his traps. Baptiste's trap-line starts at his log cabin in the woods, and runs in a rough circle. As he follows it, it takes him a good many miles from his cabin, and then brings him home again. Here is a little diagram of the trap-line.

By courtesy of Canadian Official News Bureau

Two trappers and their dogs at one of the shacks on their trap-line

The diagram shows that at two places along the trap-line there are small shacks. The cabin and the two shacks are each a day's journey apart.

Baptiste is heading down the trail towards the first shack. His dogs are trotting on ahead, dragging a sledge behind them. The sledge is partly loaded with bait for Baptiste's traps. There are some frozen fish, some smoked deer meat, some freshly killed rabbits, and several other kinds of bait, for different kinds of animals like different kinds of food.

Baptiste visits each trap in turn along the line. Wherever he finds an animal that has been caught, he removes it from the trap, and if it is not already dead, he kills it at once. He ties the animal on to the sledge, puts fresh bait in the trap, and then goes on to the next trap on the line.

Just before dark, Baptiste and his dogs reach the first shack. In the shack there is a good supply of firewood and food. Baptiste soon has a roaring fire going in the stove, and a good hearty meal cooking on top. The dogs have curled up in the snow outside the shack. For their supper Baptiste gives them frozen fish.

During the next day, Baptiste follows the trap-line to the second shack, where he spends the second night. Then, on the third day, he covers the last lap of the line,

By courtesy of Canadian National Railways

How Baptiste catches fish in the winter-time

visit his traps as often as possible. His days at home are as busy as his days "on the line", for he has to skin the animals of the last catch, and get bait for the next trip. Getting bait means that Baptiste must spend many a cold hour fishing through the ice on a lake near his cabin, or hunting rabbits and other small animals with his gun.

Many of the trappers in the North Woods of Canada are young men whose homes are on farms farther south. They go north in the autumn, spend the winter trapping, and come back in the spring with their catch of pelts. Many other trappers live in the North Woods all the time, as Baptiste does. Some of these men are Red Indians, and others, like Baptiste, are French-Canadians.

In Eurasia the best trapping-grounds are in Siberia, for in northern Europe the wild animals have been killed off so fast that they are not nearly so plentiful as they once were. The Siberian trappers belong to many different groups of rather dark-skinned people.

and reaches home by supper-time. Sometimes, though, he is caught in a blinding snowstorm, and has to stay several days in one of the shacks.

If his luck is good, Baptiste reaches home with several foxes, a good many martens and minks, and perhaps a lynx or a wolf.

Every trapper knows how to skin the animals so that the pelts come off in perfect shape. They must be taken from the animals carefully so that none of the edges will be torn or ragged, and then they must be stretched and dried.

Baptiste is seldom at home more than a day or two at a time during the trapping season, for he must

But no matter who the trappers are, or whether they live and work in America or Eurasia, they all make their living in the same way. All through the long, cold winter they trudge through the snow, fighting blizzards and bitter winds, to get their catch of wild animals.

By courtesy of the Hudson's Bay Company

Here is a Canadian trapper with part of his winter's catch of pelts

Week by week, each trapper adds to his stock of pelts. If the animals are plentiful and the trapping is good, a single trapper may have several hundred fine pelts before the winter is over.

Baptiste, you will remember, sells his pelts at a trading-station on the shore of Hudson Bay. Scattered here and there through the lonely stretches of the North Woods there are many such stations where the trappers sell their winter catch of furs. The selling is done in the spring, after the ice on the streams has melted away. Many of the Canadian trappers travel long distances in their canoes to reach the nearest trading-station.

It is much the same in Siberia. Scattered far and wide along the rivers of the great Siberian forest are small towns and villages to which the trappers bring their furs in the spring, and where they buy supplies before going back to their lonely homes in the wilderness.

The men who buy the pelts are employed by great fur companies. They send the pelts to certain large cities in America, Europe, and Asia. We call these cities fur markets because they are centres where furs are sold wholesale to the makers of fur garments in many parts of the world. London is one of these great fur markets, and Montreal, the chief port of Canada, is another.

By courtesy of the Hudson's Bay Company

Two little Red Indians whose father is a trapper in the North Woods of Canada

The next time you see a shop window filled with fur coats, perhaps you will think of Baptiste and the other trappers of the northern forests. Can you picture them going the rounds of their trap-lines in the cold, snowy winter, and paddling down the streams to sell their pelts in the spring? If you can, you will never forget that fur-trapping is one of the very few ways in which people can make a living in the cold northern forests.

Some things to do

1. Draw pictures of some of the wild animals of the northern forests. Tell what you know of their habits.

2. Explain why the pelts of so many of these animals are wanted by people in countries like our own.

3. Explain why the trapping is done in the winter-time.

4. Pretend that you are a fur-trapper and tell about your work.

MILL TOWNS AND LOGGING CAMPS

The greater part of the northern forest of North America is in Canada, but it extends southwards into both the north-western and north-eastern parts of the United States. The northern forest of Eurasia is shared by four countries—Norway, Sweden, Finland, and the Soviet Union. Perhaps you know that the Soviet Union is the largest country in the world. Within it is the part of Europe which we call Russia, and all of Siberia, in Asia.

If you were to visit the southern parts of the forests in Norway, Sweden, Finland, or Russia, you would find a good many towns where there are sawmills and pulp-mills. In the sawmills giant saws slice the trunks of trees into boards. In the pulp-mills logs are chopped to bits and ground to make wood-pulp.

Wood-pulp has two very important uses. One is for the making of paper, and the other is for the making of rayon, or artificial silk. The paper in this book is made of wood-pulp that came from Sweden.

Northern Europe is not the only part of the world where you could visit settlements which have grown up round sawmills and pulp-mills. There are many in southern Canada and northern United States, and a few along the southern margin of the forest in Siberia.

By courtesy of the Swedish Travel Bureau

How one of the sawmill towns in Sweden looks from an aeroplane

Nearly all these settlements are on the banks of rivers. Some of them are good-sized towns, but most of them are rather small. Some are no more than villages, where nearly all the men work in the sawmills or the pulp-mills.

The picture gives you a good idea of one of these towns. Notice the logs floating in the river, and the great stacks of boards on the opposite bank. The ship has come up the river from the sea to take on a cargo of lumber.

Wherever you find settlements of this kind, you may be sure that there are logging camps in the forests beyond. The logging camps are places in the woods where men are busy cutting down trees and sawing them into logs. Another name for logging is "lumbering", and the men who do it are called lumbermen. Some of the camps are fairly near the mill towns. Others are deep in the forest, many miles away.

Let us pretend that it is mid-winter, and that we are visiting a logging camp in Sweden. We have on our warmest clothes, for the weather is bitterly cold, and the snow lies deep on the ground.

The logging camp is a little cluster of long, low buildings made of logs. One of them is the kitchen and dining-room of the camp. The others are the houses where the lumbermen sleep. All of them are

A 8

roughly built, as if the men did not expect to use them for very long.

Perhaps you can think why a logging camp is such a rough and un-finished-looking place. It is because the buildings are used only so long as the men are cutting down trees in that particular neighbourhood. After all the full-grown trees have been cut, the lumbermen are sent to another place in the forest and a new camp is built for them there.

A number of well-trodden paths in the snow lead away from the camp in different directions. Any one of them will take us to a place in the woods where some of the lumbermen are at work.

It is a wonderful sight to see two men fell a tall, strong tree. First they cut a deep notch in one side of the trunk with their axes. Then they pick up a big saw with a handle at each end. One man takes one end of the saw, and the other man the other end. Together they saw through the thick trunk from the side opposite the notch.

Suddenly, as the blade nears the notch, there is a sharp, splintering noise. With a shout of warning, the men drop the saw and jump out of the way. For a moment the tall tree sways and quivers. Then with a snapping, crackling crash, it falls headlong to the ground.

As soon as a tree is down, other men attack it with axes and saws. First they cut off the branches. Then they cut the trunk into logs by sawing it crosswise in several places.

Other groups of lumbermen are doing the same work at safe distances from one another. Tree after tree comes crashing down to lose its branches and be sawn into logs. Day after day and week after week, the work goes on until all the full-grown trees have been felled and only the young ones left to grow.

Meanwhile, other workmen are busy taking the logs to the nearest river. They use large sledges drawn by horses or motor-tractors. On the banks of the river the men roll the logs off the sledges. The river is frozen over now, but when spring comes, the ice will melt. Then the logs will be rolled into the water and the swift current will carry them down-stream to a sawmill or a pulp-mill.

By courtesy of Canadian Official News Bureau
Loading a sledge with logs in Canada

In some places railways have been built to carry the logs to the mills. In such places the lumbering can be done at any time of the year. Far more logs, however, go floating down the streams, for this is the cheapest way of getting them to the mills. In the places where the streams are used, most of the lumbering is done in the winter. That is because it is so much easier to haul the logs over the snow to the river-banks than to haul them over bare, rough ground.

What you have seen at a logging camp in Sweden, you could see at all the other logging camps in the countries which share the northern forests. In the spring many of the rivers in these wooded regions are filled with logs. As the logs are swept downstream by the current, they crowd and jostle one another. Sometimes they become wedged together so tightly that the whole stream is blocked.

Lumbermen call this kind of accident a "log-jam". The logs stick fast until the men run out on them and pry them apart with long poles. Breaking a log-jam is hard, dangerous work, and it often takes a long time to loosen the "key log" which is causing all the trouble.

SOME THINGS TO REMEMBER ABOUT THE NORTHERN FORESTS

In the cold northern forests, as in the dry lands, there are a few places where the mining of iron ore, copper, and other metals has led to the growth of scattered settlements. For example, there are mining towns in south-eastern Canada. Mining, trapping, and lumbering are the three principal ways in which people can earn a living in these lands where so little farming can be carried on.

By courtesy of the Swedish Travel Bureau
Hauling logs to the banks of a stream in Sweden

By courtesy of Canadian National Railways
The beginning of a log-jam in a Canadian river

The reason why people can earn a living by these occupations is that ores, furs, and wood are the products of these regions which are needed by people in other places. Of the three, the wood is the most necessary, and work connected with it provides a living for the most people.

There are forests in many other parts of the world, but more trees are cut for lumber and pulp-wood in the northern forests than anywhere else. There are some interesting reasons for this which you will like to know.

Remember that to the south of the northern forests there are warmer lands which are much better suited for farming. Many of these lands are crowded with people. Millions of the people live and work in cities and towns. Millions of others live and work on farms.

Wherever there are large numbers of people, there is need of wood for many different purposes. You yourself can name a great many ways in which we use wood in our own crowded country.

Once upon a time the lands south of the northern forests had plenty of trees of their own. Because these lands were so good for farming, more and more people came to live in them. Little by little the trees were cut down to clear land for crops and to supply wood for building and other purposes. To-day most of the forests in these lands have been destroyed, and the people must now get most of their wood from outside.

Now it happens that the trees in the northern forests are of the kinds most needed for lumber and pulp-wood. They are mostly pines, spruces, hemlocks, firs, and other evergreen trees which do not shed their leaves in winter.

The wood of the northern evergreens is strong, yet it is soft enough to be cut and sawn easily. That is why it makes good lumber. For pulp-wood there is nothing better than northern spruce and hemlock.

You can understand now why there are many logging camps and many mill towns in the southern parts of these forests. It is because the northern forests can supply the kinds of wood which are needed in such large quantities in the crowded lands to the south.

A lonely settlement in the wilderness of the great Canadian forest

Royal Canadian Air Force Photograph

Altogether, the logging camps and the sawmills, pulp-mills, and mines provide work for many thousands of people. Remember, though, that the forests cover huge stretches of land. Remember, too, that most of the logging camps and the mining and mill towns are in the southern parts of the forests—the parts nearest the crowded lands where metals and wood are needed. Elsewhere in the northern forests, few mines have ever been opened, and few trees have ever been cut.

So, as a whole, the northern forests have only a few people. They are lands of widely scattered settlements and lonely trappers' cabins. Like the dry lands, they are thinly populated because they offer so few ways in which people can make a living. We may be almost certain that they will always remain largely a lonely wilderness of trees and streams.

Some things to do

1. Pretend that you are a lumberman, and tell about your work.
2. Say whether you would rather be a lumberman or a trapper, and why.
3. Explain why logging camps do not become permanent settlements in the forests.

Some questions about the northern forests

1. Why do the lands covered by the northern forests have long, cold winters and short, cool summers?
2. Why haven't the trees been cut down to clear the land for farming?
3. How do the trees and the wild animals help people to make a living in these forests?
4. Why are the settlements for the most part trading towns, mining towns, and mill towns?
5. What would you say is the principal reason why the northern forests of Eurasia and North America are among the most thinly populated regions of the world?

61

By courtesy of Booth Line

A glimpse of the tropical forest and some native huts along the Amazon River

3. THE TROPICAL FORESTS
MAP DISCOVERIES

Do you know what people mean when they speak of the "tropical lands"? If you don't, you can easily find out by looking at the maps on pages 22-23.

Find the line marked "Tropic of Cancer", and then the line marked "Tropic of Capricorn". Notice that the Tropic of Capricorn is the same distance south of the Equator as the Tropic of Cancer is north of the Equator.

Like the Equator and the Arctic and Antarctic circles, the two tropics are lines drawn on maps and globes, not real lines on the earth itself. If you have a globe in your schoolroom, trace both tropics on it. This will show you that the tropics run east and west round the globe, forming circles like the Equator and the Arctic and Antarctic circles.

The tropics are useful lines because they mark the northern and southern margins of the warm belt of the earth. This belt forms a broad zone, or band, round the middle of the earth on both sides of the Equator. It is often called the *torrid zone*, which means the "hot zone".

You can understand now what we mean by the tropical lands. They are the lands between the tropics, or the lands of the torrid zone. Tropical lowlands are hot the whole year round, but tropical highlands are cool. Later we shall learn the reasons for this.

Some Amazon Indians paddling on the river in their dug-out canoe

A Trip up the Amazon River

If you will look at Maps III and IV at the back of the book, you will see that there are large forests in the basin of the Amazon River in South America and in the basin of the Congo River in Africa. The basin of a river is the land drained by the river itself and all the tributary streams which flow into it.

We call these forests of the Amazon Basin and the Congo Basin " tropical forests ". They cover great stretches of tropical land which is low enough to be warm all the year round.

Let us pretend that we are on a cargo boat steaming up the Amazon River from the Atlantic Ocean. No matter what month it may be, the weather is sure to be hot, and the air is so moist that the heat is hard to bear. We feel very lazy, as all white people do when they go to the hot, rainy parts of the tropical lands.

Hour after hour our boat ploughs the muddy waters of the great river. For miles and miles all we see is the river itself and the thick growth of trees along the nearer bank. The river is so broad that we can hardly see the opposite bank.

Here and there we pass a little cluster of grass-roofed huts in a clearing on the river-bank. Only at widely-scattered points are there any towns, and they are small. Nowhere do we see any roads or railways, but now and then we pass a dug-out canoe paddled by dark-skinned natives. The great forest is a quiet, lonely region.

By courtesy of Booth Line

How a tropical jungle looks on a sunny day

shuts out all the sunlight from the forest floor.

In other parts of the tropical forests the leafy canopy is not so thick, and the sunlight filters through to the forest floor. In these parts, which are called "jungles", the ground between the trees is covered with such a tangle of plants and vines that a person cannot get through it without using a hatchet to cut his way.

The boat on which we are travelling is bound for Manaos, the only large town of the great Amazon forest. The hold is filled with cotton goods and other things to be delivered at Manaos, and the captain has orders to take on a cargo of rubber and brazil-nuts for the return trip to Great Britain.

It will take two or three days for the boat to be unloaded and loaded again. Meanwhile, we shall have a chance to learn a little about the people of the Amazon forest and how they live.

Most of the people are either South American Indians or *mestizos*. The mestizos are of mixed Indian and Portuguese blood. They are descendants of white men who came to South America from Portugal long ago and married Indian women.

The weather is what we should call "muggy" at home, for the air is both warm and moist. Nearly every day there are heavy showers. The rain pours down in torrents from dark, puffy clouds, and when it stops and the sun comes out again, the air seems hotter and steamier than ever.

Look at the lower map on page 11, and you will see that the Amazon Basin is one of the rainiest lands in the world. The Congo Basin, too, is a warm, rainy land.

It is because of the heat and the rain that these two river basins are covered with such a thick growth of trees. Many of the trees are large, straight, and very tall. Where such trees grow close together, the meeting of their branches high overhead forms a thick canopy of leaves that

If we were to go exploring in the depths of the Amazon forest, we should find scattered groups of Indians who make their living entirely by hunting and fishing. They know little or nothing about the outside world, and some of them are savage and unfriendly.

Most of the people, however, live in scattered settlements along the Amazon and its tributaries, and do a little farming. Their houses, as we have seen, are thatched-roofed huts. Where the river-banks are low, the huts stand on stilts six or eight feet above the ground. This is to keep them safe in times of flood, when the water rises in the rivers and overflows the banks.

Round the little settlements are small gardens where the women grow manioc, maize, bananas, and a few vegetables. Manioc is a root which is grated and roasted to make a pasty kind of flour. For the rest of their food the forest people depend mostly on turtles and fish that they catch in the rivers.

By courtesy of Booth Line

Shooting fish with a bow and arrow is a native way of getting food from the Amazon

Something to do

Use the maps on pages 22-23 in answering these questions.

1. Which of the two continents of the Western Hemisphere has more tropical land?

2. Which continent in the Eastern Hemisphere has the most tropical land?

3. Has Europe any tropical land?

Some things to explain

1. Explain what a river basin is.

2. Suppose a Canadian trapper were to ask you how the forests of the Amazon and Congo basins differ from the northern forests, and why. What would you say?

3. Suppose he were to ask you why the weather in the Congo and Amazon basins is warm all the year round. How would you explain that fact?

By courtesy of Booth Line

A mestizo boy of the Amazon forest. He is standing under a banana tree

By courtesy of Booth Line   Pan-American Union

This is Piru's home in the Amazon forest, and here is Piru himself gathering latex

A Day with a Rubber-Gatherer

Suppose we spend one day of our stay in the Amazon forest visiting one of the mestizo families. The father of this family is named Piru, and he is a rubber-gatherer. That means that he collects the milky juice from the rubber trees which grow wild in the Amazon forest. The juice is called *latex*.

Early in the morning Piru leaves his hut carrying some small tin cups and a sharp knife. He follows a path that leads into the thick forest. Presently he comes to a tall rubber tree. He cuts several gashes in the bark of the tree with his knife, and hangs a cup under each gash. Then on he goes along the narrow path to the next rubber tree, which may be some distance away.

Piru's path from one rubber tree to another is rather like Baptiste's trap-line in the Great North Woods. It winds through the forest and brings him home again. It doesn't take him so far, though, for Piru always gets home for his mid-day meal with his family.

In the afternoon Piru starts out again, this time carrying a big tin bucket. He goes over the same route from tree to tree. He finds each little cup filled with latex which has oozed from the gash that he made in the morning. He empties each cup of latex into his bucket, and by the time he reaches home the bucket is full.

The latex that Piru collects each day is pure liquid rubber. Before he can sell it, he must make it into big, hard balls. You would be interested to watch him as he does this work.

On the earth floor of his hut he builds a fire of bark and nuts. Over the fire he places a little metal chimney which is large at the bottom and tapers to a small hole at the top. Over the hole is a pole held up at each end by a notched stick.

With a home-made ladle Piru pours a little latex on the part of the pole above the chimney-top. Instead of running off, the latex thickens and hardens in the smoke and heat from the chimney. In a few minutes Piru turns the pole and pours on a little more latex.

By courtesy of Mrs. M. C. Fambec

Children in the Amazon forest help in making balls of rubber from the latex

Piru works this way for hours, building a ball of rubber round the pole by pouring on a little latex at a time. If he gets tired, one of the children takes a turn at the work. When they have built a ball of rubber big enough to sell, they slip it off the pole and start another.

The rubber is bought by traders who call at the villages in motor boats. They take it to Manaos and other towns along the Amazon, where cargo boats pick it up and carry it away to distant lands.

Many of the Indians and mestizos are rubber-gatherers like Piru. Others are gatherers of brazil-nuts. Very likely you have eaten brazil-nuts, for many of them are sold in Britain. They are really the seeds of a large round fruit. The fruit grows on one of the tallest of the many kinds of trees in the Amazon forest.

Brazil-nuts and rubber are the only products of any importance which people in the outside world want from the Amazon forest. The natives are paid for collecting them, and with the money they buy cotton cloth for clothing and the few tools and other things that they need.

Something to do

Explain how Piru's life in the Amazon forest of South America is different from Baptiste's life in the North Woods of Canada, and why.

Photo: E.N.A.   Photo : P. Hoefler

A pygmy family outside their tiny hut and some pygmy men with their bows and arrows

THE CONGO FOREST

If you were to visit the Congo forest in central Africa, you would see many things that would remind you of the Amazon forest in South America. A few roads have been built in the Congo forest, and a few short lines of railway, but travel is chiefly by boat on the Congo River and its tributaries. Most of the people live in small villages of thatched-roofed huts scattered along the streams, and only here and there are there any good-sized trading towns.

Hidden away in the very depths of the Congo forest are a few groups of strange little people called pygmies. They are dark-skinned and very small, and they wear little or no clothing. They know nothing about farming, and they get their food by hunting and by gathering nuts and fruits that grow wild in the forest.

Pygmy settlements are so small that they cannot even be called villages. Just a few families (seldom more than six) live together in small open spaces in the forest. For each family there is a tiny round hut built of bent branches and covered with big leaves.

The pygmy men are very skilful hunters. They have no guns, but they are splendid shots with bows and arrows and with spears. They are brave little fellows, too, and not afraid of hunting savage animals.

The pygmies are really nomads of the forest, for they move from place to place in search of game. Whenever they move to a new spot in the forest, they build new huts for shelter from the rain.

The Congo forest is a very large region, and the pygmies live in only one portion of it. Most of the native people are Negroes, and they live in much the same way as the natives of the Amazon forest. The women grow food crops in little garden patches round the river-side villages. The men add to the food-supply by hunting and fishing.

On their hunting-trips the men sometimes kill an elephant, and when they do, they sell the tusks to traders in the towns. You probably know that elephant tusks give us ivory. Elephants, however, are becoming rather scarce in the Congo forest, and the Negroes do not get so many tusks as they once did.

Palm kernels are the chief product which the Negroes collect for trading. The trees from which they come are called oil-palms, and they grow wild in the Congo forest. The kernels are the seeds of the fruit of the oil-palms. The Negroes cut the big bunches of fruit from the trees, remove the kernels, and dry them in the sun. Then they put the dried kernels in their dug-out canoes and carry them to the trading-stations along the Congo and its tributaries.

Large quantities of palm kernels are wanted in countries like Britain for the oil that can be pressed out of them. The oil is used chiefly in the making of soap and candles.

By courtesy of United Christian Missionary Society

Here are the tusks of about fifteen elephants at a trading-station in the Congo forest

So, you see, the people of the two greatest tropical forests in the world live in much the same way. When you think of these forests, remember that they are lands where the settlements are scattered along the streams. Remember, too, that there are miles and miles of almost trackless forest, with no roads or railways, and with only a few narrow footpaths.

Can you explain

1. Why the people of the Congo forest and the Amazon forest live and work in much the same way?

2. Why they live and work so differently from the people of the northern forests?

WHY THE TROPICAL FORESTS ARE NOT THICKLY POPULATED

Do you wonder why the tropical forests of Africa and South America haven't more people? There are a number of interesting reasons.

Photo : Sport and General

A rubber plantation on land where tropical jungle has been cleared away

To begin with, the tropical forests are not easy places for carrying on farming, and without a good deal of farming there cannot be food enough for large numbers of people. Can you think of any reasons why farming is difficult in these regions?

Remember that if forest-land is to be turned into good land for farming, all the trees must be cut down. In the tropical forests the trees grow so close together and are so tangled with vines that clearing even one acre of land takes a long time and a great deal of hard work.

Then, too, there are other troubles. Weeds grow so fast in the heat and dampness that if left to themselves, they will very soon choke the crops in a field or garden. Worse than that, the soils in tropical forests are for the most part rather poor, and after being used for a few years, they no longer produce good crops.

So, you see, farming is far from easy in these warm, rainy lands. The natives do not try to cut down the larger trees when they want land for a garden. They simply clear away the smaller trees and the tangle of plants and vines on the ground. Then they plant their crops in little patches among the trees. When the soil is worn out in one of these little clearings, they stop using it and make a new garden somewhere else.

In a few parts of the Amazon and Congo basins there are large farms called plantations, where crops such as bananas, cacao (from which cocoa and chocolate are made), rubber trees, and oil-palms are grown.

Plantation farming is successful because the plantations are owned and managed by business companies made up of white men. The companies have money enough to clear large tracts of land and to keep the soil in good condition by enriching it with fertilizers. They hire native labourers for all the outdoor work.

Compared with the numbers of natives in the Congo and Amazon basins, there are very few white people. The principal reason for this is the weather. The constant heat and dampness are unhealthy for white people, and in addition, there is always the chance of catching dangerous fevers spread by mosquitoes and other insects.

Perhaps you wonder why there are not a good many logging camps in the Amazon and Congo forests as there are in some parts of the northern forests. One reason is that logging is much more difficult in the tropical forests. You can easily imagine how hard it is to cut down the trees in their tangle of vines, and to get the logs out to the streams.

A more important reason is that people in the outside world do not need very large quantities of wood from these forests. Tropical woods are beautifully grained, and they are used for making expensive furniture and panelling. But for general building purposes, for which much greater quantities of lumber are needed, tropical woods are too hard and too costly.

Of course you have seen furniture made of mahogany, and you may have seen teak, ebony, or rosewood used in one way or another. These are the tropical woods that are most often used. They come to us chiefly from Burma, Siam, the Guinea coast of Africa, and the West Indies,

Photo: Dorien Leigh

Does this picture help you to see why logging in the tropical forests is not easy?

where the trees are cut fairly near the ports from which the logs are shipped away. Our need for such woods, however, is small compared with our need for the softer woods from the northern forests.

You are ready now to sum up the reasons why the Amazon forest and the Congo forest are not thickly populated, and why they are lands of scattered settlements.

Remember that farming in these regions is not easy. The best the natives can do is to grow just enough food in their little gardens

Photo : P. Hoefler

A passenger-and-cargo boat on the " main highway " in the Congo Basin

to live on. Even with fish from the streams and meat from wild animals, the food-supply is not great enough for very large numbers of people.

If there were a great many products of the Amazon and Congo basins which were wanted by people in the outside world, there would be work for many more people of the dark-skinned races there. But the list of things which people outside really need and want from these regions is small, and the collecting of them does not require enough work to support large numbers of people.

It is easy to understand why the people of these two great forests live in scattered settlements along the streams. Think how hard it is to get about on land in a region where there are scarcely any roads, and where, in many places, even a path must be hacked out with a hatchet !

You may think of the two principal rivers — the Amazon and the Congo — as the main highways into these forest regions from the sea, and of their tributary streams as the side roads. Naturally, most of the people wish to live where they can use these waterways for getting from place to place. That is why the settlements are scattered along the banks of the streams, and why vast stretches of forest-land between the streams have hardly any people.

Some questions about the tropical forests

1. In which continents are the two greatest tropical forests of the world situated ?

2. Why is one called the Congo forest and the other the Amazon forest ?

3. Why are they unhealthy regions for white people ?

4. Why are they difficult regions in which to use the land for farming ?

5. Why are they regions in which lumbering is not very important ?

6. How do the native people make their living ?

7. Why do they need less clothing and shelter than the people of the northern forests ?

8. What forest products do the natives collect and sell to traders ? What becomes of these products ?

9. Why are most of the settlements in these forests situated along the rivers ?

10. What would you say are the principal reasons why the tropical forests are not thickly populated ?

Photo : Stump & Co.

Would you like to live in a valley like this, with high mountains all about you ?

4. THE MOUNTAINOUS LANDS

Have you ever spent a holiday in the Lake District of England, or in Wales, or in the Scottish Highlands ? If you have, or if by chance you live in one of those regions, you know that mountainous lands are very rough lands.

Mountainous lands are really lands of mountains and valleys. The higher parts are the mountains, and the lower lands among them are the valleys. In some mountainous lands the mountains are grouped in lines called *ranges*, and the valleys between them are long and narrow. Other mountainous lands are an irregular jumble of mountains and valleys.

Ben Nevis, in the Scottish Highlands, is the highest mountain in Great Britain. Its peak, or top, is 4406 feet above the sea. Sea-level, or the surface of the sea, is the starting-place for measuring the height of all land, everywhere in the world.

There are a number of peaks in the Scottish Highlands that are more than 4000 feet above sea-level, and 4000 feet is nearly four-fifths of a mile. That may seem very high to you, but compared with many of the mountainous lands of the world, the Scottish Highlands are low.

Take, for example, the Himalaya Mountains in Asia, which are the highest mountains in the world.

73

A glimpse of the farm-lands in the high valley in the Andes where Quito is situated

Photo: G. C. Sanderson

The highest peaks there are more than five miles above the level of the sea. Or take the long ranges of the Andes Mountains in South America. The highest peaks there are about four miles above sea-level.

So, you see, there are great differences in height among the mountainous lands of the world. But whether they are high, or rather low, they all *seem* high to anyone looking at them from the lower ground. For that reason we say that all mountains are high lands.

The most important thing to remember about mountainous lands is their rough surface. In travelling over them on foot, on a bicycle, or in a motor-car, one seems always to be going up or down. Only where there are long valleys between the mountain ranges are there any places where roads or paths are level for any great distance.

SOME COOL LANDS WITHIN THE TROPICS

If you could follow the line of the Equator straight across South America from east to west, you would travel for about seventeen hundred miles over the very low land of the Amazon Basin. You already know how hot you would find it there.

Then you would begin to climb. In the next three hundred miles of your journey you would climb to a high valley between two ranges of the Andes in Ecuador. At the town of Quito, your journey's end, you would be more than 9000 feet above the level of the sea.

How different this high Andean valley is from the hot, steamy Amazon lowland! The days are cool and spring-like all the year round, and the nights are always very chilly. The farming folk grow wheat, barley, and other crops of the kinds that are grown in the cooler lands beyond the tropics. They rear cattle, too, and cattle are animals which cannot stand the heat and moisture of tropical lowlands.

It is easy to see that tropical highlands are quite different from tropical lowlands. They are much cooler, and if they are very high, they are very cold. From Quito you can see the beautiful mountain peak called Cotopaxi, which means "shining height". Cotopaxi is so high that its peak is always covered with a cap of ice and snow.

Do you know why highlands in the warm belt of the earth are cool or cold? It is simply because they *are* highlands. Anyone who has ever made a high flight in an aeroplane will tell you that the higher he went, the cooler the air became.

The warmth in the air grows less and less as one rises higher and higher above the level of the sea. Mountain-tops everywhere are much

By courtesy of Grace Line

One of the snow-capped peaks of the Andes in the tropical part of South America

cooler than the lower land round the mountain bases. So, even in the torrid zone, there are cool lands, and in the highest parts of that zone there are even very cold lands.

If you will look at the upper map on page 11, you will see that there are more people living in the tropical part of the Andes Mountains than in most parts of the Amazon lowland. You can easily understand why. It is because the weather in tropical highlands is so much pleasanter and more healthy than the weather in tropical lowlands.

Some things to do

1. Write a sentence or two telling how mountainous lands are different from plains.

2. Say which of these two kinds of lands you think is better for farming, and why you think so.

3. See if you can explain clearly why there are cool lands, and even cold lands, in the tropical belt of the earth.

Photo : G. C. Sanderson

A corner of one of the market-places in Quito

Photo: Dorien Leigh

A train coming through a narrow gorge in the Rocky Mountains

A Glimpse of the Rocky Mountains

Let us imagine that we are in the Rocky Mountains of North America. The Rockies include the highest mountains of that continent. Many of the peaks are higher than the highest ones in the Alps in Europe.

If it is winter, we shall find snow everywhere, even in the lowest valleys. If it is summer, we shall find the valleys green, and only the highest peaks and slopes white with snow. In the valleys we shall see farmers at work in their grain-fields and orchards, and looking after their cattle and other farm animals.

If we climb one of the mountains, we shall first pass through a belt of thick forest. We may see a logging camp, with lumbermen busily at work felling trees, not far above the valley floor. There may be a saw-mill just below, and if so, we shall see the logs sliding down a wooden chute into a pond by the mill.

As we climb higher, the trees thin out and become more and more stunted. We are now getting near the " tree-line "—a height where the winters are so long and cold that trees cannot grow there. It is rather like going northwards from the northern forest to the tundra.

As we leave the trees behind, we come out into a high valley covered with green grass. Round about it rise the higher mountain slopes, bare and rocky. Up here we shall see thousands of sheep tended by shepherds who live in waggons during the summer. These high mountain pastures are summer feeding-grounds for sheep from farms in the valleys.

If you are a good climber, perhaps you can climb to the top of one of the highest peaks. You will need a guide, though, and spiked shoes, for as you near the mountain-top you will have to walk over ice and crusted snow. You may even have to climb up one of those very slowly creeping " rivers of ice " that we call glaciers. If you do, you will be roped to your guide so that, if you fall into one of the deep cracks in the ice, he can pull you out.

The pastures where the sheep feed in the summer are no higher than the valleys in the tropical part of the Andes where many people live all the year round, growing crops and rearing cattle. But here in the Rockies no one can live all the year round on the high pasture-lands. Perhaps you can think why.

It is because the Rocky Mountains are well outside the tropics. They are in the belt of the earth which we call the *north temperate zone*. This is the belt which lies between the Tropic of Cancer and the Arctic Circle. In the Southern Hemisphere there is another belt of the same kind, between the Tropic of Capricorn and the Antarctic Circle. We call that belt the *south temperate zone*.

In the temperate zones, the lowlands are warm in summer, and cool or cold in winter. The high-

lands are cooler than the lowlands in summer, and very cold in the winter. For this reason the people who live among the mountains of the temperate zones choose for their

homes the lower valleys. Living in the higher valleys would be much like living in the Arctic tundra.

By courtesy of W. W. Atwood

Summer pasture for sheep above the tree-line in the Rocky Mountains

WHY THE SETTLEMENTS IN MOUNTAINOUS LANDS ARE SCATTERED

Maps I and II at the front of the book will show you that there are mountainous lands in every continent. There are many differences among these lands, but in one way they are all alike. In every one of them most of the towns and villages are in the valleys. Often the mountain ranges that separate the valleys from one another are almost uninhabited.

You can easily understand why the valleys are the best places for people to live in. It is hard to build

Photo : Keystone

A town in the Rocky Mountains which has grown up round a silver mine

a town on a steep mountain-side, and hard to build roads to reach it. Then, too, it isn't easy to do any farming where slopes are as steep as they are on mountain-sides.

So, in most mountainous lands, the towns and villages are strung along the valleys where it is easiest to build roads and railways, and where there is level land for growing crops. If the mountain-sides are used at all, it is chiefly as pasture-lands for cattle, sheep, or goats.

If there are towns or villages perched on the mountain-sides, they often prove to be mining centres. Many mountain lands are rich in ores of gold, silver, copper, lead, or zinc, and wherever a large mine is opened, a settlement of miners and other workers grows up around it.

As a whole, mountainous lands are not very thickly populated. This will not surprise you if you stop to think how much of the land is too steep for farming, and how much harder it is to get about over the rough surface of mountains than over the smoother surface of plains.

There are, however, a few countries which are largely mountainous and yet have a great many people. One of these countries is Switzerland, in Europe. Another is Japan, a country of mountainous islands off the eastern coast of Asia.

But even in the most thickly populated of these countries, it is only the valleys among the mountains and the lowlands along their borders that are crowded with towns, villages, and farms. In such countries the people have found a way of using some of the lower mountain slopes for growing crops. The picture on the next page shows how they do it.

This method of using steep slopes for growing crops is called " terracing ". Terraces are like giant steps cut into the mountain-side. Each one provides a strip of level land for crops, and across the front a wall is built to keep the outer edge from crumbling and the soil from sliding downhill.

It takes a great deal of hard work to build terraces and to keep them in repair. But in mountainous lands where the valleys are very crowded with people, this is the only way of getting additional land for farming.

Most of the mountainous lands, however, are not crowded enough for terracing to be necessary. In Switzerland, for example, there are terraces for vineyards in some places, but for the most part the lower mountain slopes are covered with forests. The upper slopes, above the tree-line, are used only as summer pastures for the cattle from the farms in the valleys.

Perhaps when you are grown up you will visit some of the mountainous countries of the world. You will then see for yourself that they are lands where the settlements are in scattered groups, and that each group of settlements occupies one of the valley lowlands.

Netherlands Indies Information Bureau

Hill-sides terraced for rice-fields in Java

Map questions

Use the maps on pages 22-23 in answering these questions.

1. In which zone of the earth are the British Isles situated?

2. Which three continents are for the most part in that same zone?

3. In which zone is most of Africa situated?

4. In which zone are South Africa and the southern parts of Australia and South America?

5. Which continent has no land in the torrid zone?

Some questions about mountainous lands

1. What is the difference between a mountain range and a mountain peak?

2. Why are some mountain peaks snow-capped the whole year through?

3. Why can people live in very high valleys among the mountains of the torrid zone?

4. Why can't people live in such high valleys among the mountains of the temperate zones?

5. What is meant by the "tree-line" on a mountain? Why are there no trees above that line?

6. How is the grassy land above the tree-line used in summer in many mountainous lands? Why isn't it used in that way all the year round?

7. Why are most of the settlements in mountainous lands situated in the valleys?

8. What would you say is the principal reason why settlements in mountainous lands are scattered?

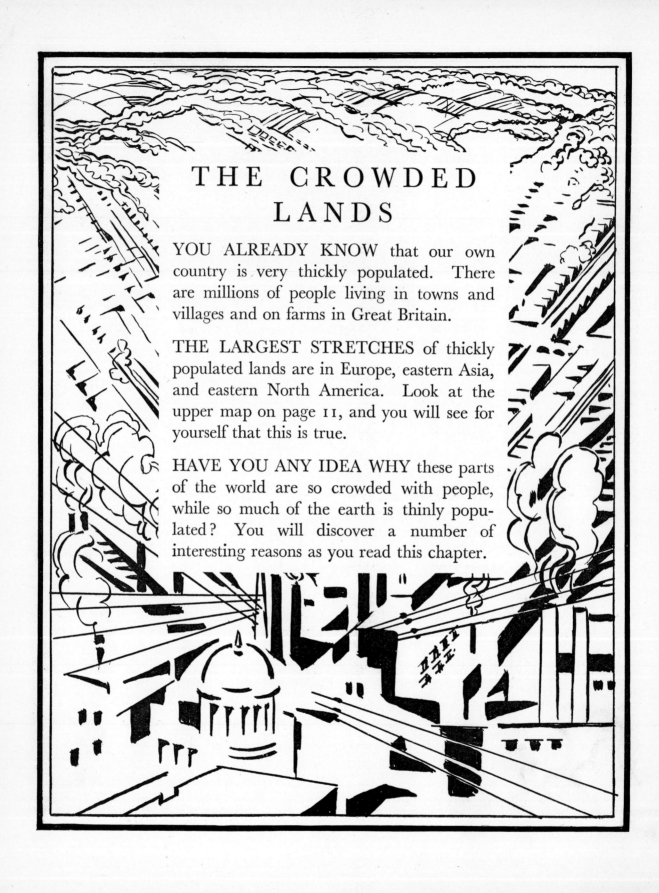

THE CROWDED LANDS

YOU ALREADY KNOW that our own country is very thickly populated. There are millions of people living in towns and villages and on farms in Great Britain.

THE LARGEST STRETCHES of thickly populated lands are in Europe, eastern Asia, and eastern North America. Look at the upper map on page 11, and you will see for yourself that this is true.

HAVE YOU ANY IDEA WHY these parts of the world are so crowded with people, while so much of the earth is thinly populated? You will discover a number of interesting reasons as you read this chapter.

In crowded Japan. All the level land round the village is used for rice-fields, and the bordering hill-sides are terraced for tea-bushes

Photo: H. G. Ponting

CHAPTER FIVE

THE CROWDED LANDS

1. THE ORIENT AND INDIA

LONG ago, when people in Europe knew much less about the world than is known to-day, they spoke of Asia as "the Orient". That was natural, for *Orient* means "east", and Asia lies to the east of Europe.

Nowadays, when we speak of the Orient, we usually mean the eastern and south-eastern parts of Asia, where China, Japan, the East Indies, and India are situated. We often speak of China and Japan as the countries of the Far East.

The upper map on page 11 shows that the Orient is crowded with people. In fact, if we add together the numbers of people living in India, the East Indies, Japan, and China, we find that they make up nearly half of all the people in the world.

Before you read further, find these countries of Asia on Map II at the front of the book. Notice that the islands of Japan and the East Indies are mountainous, but not wholly so. Along their coasts there are lowland plains, and among the mountains there are many valley lowlands.

By courtesy of N.Y.K. Line

Fujiyama always wears a cap of snow

China, too, is mountainous, as you can see from the map. But notice the patches of green which show that China has large plains in the basins of the principal rivers. Then look at India, with the broad plain of the Ganges and Indus rivers in the north, and the Deccan farther south. The Deccan is a rather hilly upland, but not much of it is too rough for farming.

It is clear from the map that in the Oriental lands, especially in India and China, there is much land that is level enough for the growing of crops. Is there also enough rain for the growth of crops? Answer this question for yourself by studying the lower map on page 11.

The answer, you see, is "yes". Except in the westernmost part of India, the Oriental lands have plenty of rain for crops. You will not be surprised, then, to learn that in these lands millions of people live and work on farms.

JAPAN AND ITS TINY FARMS

Japan is sometimes called "the Britain of the Orient". One reason for this is that Japan is an island country, lying off the eastern coast of Asia just as the British Isles lie off the western coast of Europe. Another reason is that Japan is the leading manufacturing country of Asia. Like Britain, it has coal-mines and many mills and factories.

Most visitors to Japan land at the great seaport of Yokohama. If the day is perfectly clear, they can see the snowy peak of Fujiyama, about sixty miles away. Fujiyama is what we call a volcanic peak. This means that it has been built up by great outpourings of lava, or molten rock, from deep down in the earth. Japan has many volcanic peaks among its mountains, but Fujiyama is the highest and the most beautiful.

Few visitors stop very long in Yokohama unless they have business there. Most of them go straight to Tokyo on the boat-train. Tokyo is the capital of Japan, and one of the largest cities in the world.

The main business section of Tokyo is not very different from that of any large town in Britain or Europe. The streets are lined with shops, office buildings, and hotels, and crowded with motor-cars, trams, and buses. Except for the throngs of Japanese people on the pavements and the Japanese shop-signs, there is not much to remind a visitor that he is in an Oriental country.

We know that when people come to Britain and visit only the large towns, they miss seeing much that is most beautiful and most interesting in our country. The same is true of Japan. The most beautiful scenery is in the valleys among the mountains, and some of the most interesting sights are the tiny Japanese farms. They are some of the smallest farms in all the world.

Millions of Japanese people live in the towns and cities and work in shops, offices, and factories, but far more live on farms. Visitors from countries like ours are always surprised to see how small the farms

Part of the main business section of Tokyo

are. Many a Japanese family gets all its food from a plot of land not much larger than an English farmer would use for pasturing a cow.

The first thing you would notice in the country districts is that all the land not needed for buildings or roads is used for farming. The next thing you would notice is that rice is the principal crop on nearly all the farms. The Japanese eat more rice than any other kind of food.

The rice-fields are always flooded while the plants are growing. Low ridges of earth round the fields hold the water in, and on these ridges the farmers grow a few vegetables or a little rye or barley. Farmers in our country would not think the ridges worth bothering about, but in Japan not a bit of land that can possibly produce a little food is wasted.

83

Photo: Dorien Leigh
Setting out young rice plants in the flooded fields

Photo: Keystone
A Japanese farmer threshing rice

Japanese farms are much too small for the use of any farm machines, even if the people could afford them. Many of the farmers haven't even a plough. When they prepare their land for planting rice, they let a little water into the fields, and then, day after day, they turn over the muddy earth with spades.

A farmer who can afford to buy a plough usually keeps an ox or a water-buffalo, or perhaps a small horse, to pull it. If not, a brother or a grown-up son does the work of a plough-horse.

The rice seeds are planted in seed-beds, and later the young plants are set out in the flooded fields. Every-one helps in this work, even the children. When harvest time comes, the rice is cut by hand with sickles and threshed by being beaten or trampled upon, or by being pulled through wooden rakes.

In the southern part of Japan, where the weather is warmest, the farmers grow two crops of rice on the same land each year. They plant the first crop in February or March, and harvest it in June or July. At once they plant the second crop, and this is ready for harvesting in October or November.

Farther north, the autumn is too cool for a second crop of rice to ripen properly. Here the second crop is wheat, barley, or rye, for these grains will ripen in cooler weather than rice. Between the rows of grain in their fields the farmers often plant rows of vegetables.

Wherever you go in Japan, you will find the farmers using their land for just as much of the year as the weather will allow, and taking the greatest pains to make it produce all the food it possibly can. They enrich the soil with fertilizer, and

Photo : Dorien Leigh

The kind of house in which many Japanese farmers live.
The roof is thatched with rice straw

Photo : Central Press

Cocoons spun by silkworms on
a Japanese farm

they pull out every weed that lifts its head above the ground. If the Japanese were not such patient, careful farmers, they could never make a living on such tiny farms.

On most Japanese farms there are fowls, but on very few are there any cattle or sheep. This is because nearly all the land is needed for growing food crops for the people, and very little can be spared for pasture or for growing fodder crops for animals.

In some parts of the country the hill-sides bordering the valleys are terraced for additional rice-fields. In other parts the hill-sides are planted with tea-bushes or mulberry trees. Mulberry trees, you know, supply the leaves on which silkworms are fed. Thousands of Japanese farmers rear silkworms and earn a

little money by selling the cocoons. Altogether, the production of cocoons on the farms is so great that Japan sends raw silk to all the manufacturing countries of the world.

It is easy to understand why Japanese farms are so small. It is because the country is mountainous and yet has so many people. The mountains are beautiful, but of little use for farming. Only the lowlands and their bordering hill-sides are suitable for crops, and there are so many millions of farmers that each one can have only a very small share of the land.

Fortunately, the soils are good, there is plenty of rain, and, except in the northernmost parts of the country, the weather is warm enough for two crops to be grown on each piece of land every year. If the lowlands

In one of Japan's cotton-spinning mills

Photo: N.Y.K. Line

were not so well suited for farming, we may be sure that Japan would not be one of the crowded lands of the earth. There would not be food for nearly so many people.

Even with the most careful farming of all the land suitable for that use, there is not enough food produced in Japan for all the people. The farmers can feed themselves, and many are able to grow a small surplus of grain or vegetables for sale in the towns. But there are far too many townspeople in Japan to be fed entirely on the surplus food from the farms. This is another way in which Japan is like Britain.

Go to any of the seaports of Japan and you will see how additional food-supplies are obtained. They come in ships from other countries, and the money to pay for them is earned by selling raw silk and manufactured goods in many parts of the world.

In Japan, as in Britain, the textile mills, ironworks, and many other kinds of mills and factories provide work for thousands of people. So also do the business offices where work connected with the buying of raw materials and with the shipping and selling of manufactured goods is carried on.

You can understand now why so many millions of people can live in the mountainous islands of Japan. Manufacturing, providing jobs for thousands of workers, is one reason, but careful farming of all the land fitted for that use is another and far more important one.

Some questions to answer

1. In what ways are the lowlands of Japan well suited to farming?
2. Why are Japanese farms so very small?
3. Why don't the farmers keep cattle and sheep as British farmers do?
4. What product of Japanese farms goes to manufacturing countries in many parts of the world?

Some things to do

1. Use the picture on page 81 to prove that Japanese farmers use all the land they possibly can for crops.
2. Explain why Japan is sometimes called " the Britain of the Orient ".
3. Say what you think is the principal reason why Japan is so thickly populated, and explain why you think so.

GLIMPSES OF CHINA

Much, but not all, that you have learned about Japan is true also of China. China is a much larger country, but it has about six times as many people, and its lowlands are as crowded as those of Japan.

Perhaps you know that the British island of Hong Kong is close to the southern coast of China. It is situated at the outer end of an estuary known as the Canton River. At the inner end of the estuary is the old Chinese city of Canton, one of the most interesting places in the Orient.

If you were going to visit Canton, you would land at Hong Kong. You would go from there to Canton in a small boat, for the estuary is not deep enough for large ocean ships. One of the first things you would notice would be the hundreds and hundreds of small boats moored side by side near the shore.

Photo : Planet News

Thousands of Chinese families live in boats like these on the river at Canton

In these little boats you would see Chinese families cooking and eating their meals, and Chinese babies tied with ropes to keep them from falling overboard. You would soon learn that thousands of Chinese children are born on these boats and never have any other home.

Perhaps you can think why so many people of Canton live in boats on the river. It is because the city is so crowded that there is not room for all the people to have homes on land. In many of the families both parents go ashore each day to work, leaving the older children to take care of the little ones. Other boat-families make their living by carrying goods from one place to another.

The moment you step ashore in Canton, you will know you are in an Oriental city, different in almost every way from cities in Britain and Europe. The river-side is swarming

Photo : Hugo Miller

A Chinese boat-family eating their mid-day meal

Photo : Planet News

A glimpse of some of the little shops in a crowded street in Canton

shops. Thousands of people live and work crowded into the smallest possible space.

In many of the homes, as well as in the workshops, people are busy weaving silk on hand-looms, carving ivory, stone, and wood, and making by hand jewellery, fans, lanterns, toys, and many other articles such as we see in shops that sell Chinese goods at home.

If you were to visit Shanghai instead of Canton, you would see China's greatest seaport. Shanghai is near the mouth of the Yangtze River, which is the main highway of travel into the crowded lowlands of central China.

Along the water-side in Shanghai there is one district which has broad, well-paved streets, and which looks much like a European city. Here European business and shipping companies have built large shops, warehouses, and office buildings, and fine hotels. But in the older parts of the city, where the Chinese live and work, the streets are as narrow and crowded as those in Canton.

In both Canton and Shanghai there are cotton mills and a few

with Chinese coolies, as the poorer labourers are called. They are carrying goods in baskets hung from yokes over their shoulders, in wheel-barrows, and in carts that they push or pull. Well-to-do people are riding about in rickshaws. There are taxi-cabs and lorries, but modern ways of getting about are less common than the old-fashioned Chinese ways.

Except in the chief business section of the city, most of the streets of Canton are narrow lanes, bordered by rows of little one- and two-storey houses and little shops and work-

other kinds of factories, but more manufacturing is done by hand than by machinery. Large quantities of Chinese goods are the work of skilled craftsmen in their homes or in the tiniest of workshops.

China has many large towns, but even so, it has a great many more farmers than townspeople. If you were to visit the country districts, you would find the people living in small villages and cultivating farms which are not much larger than those of the Japanese.

Like Japan, China is fortunate in having good soils in the lowlands, and plenty of rain. In the southern part of the country the weather is so warm that farming can be carried on all the year round, and, in all but the northernmost parts, at least two crops can be grown on each piece of land every year.

Chinese farmers do nearly all their work by hand just as Japanese farmers do, and they use most of their land for growing rice and other food crops. They farm with the same painstaking care as the Japanese, and for the same reason. Only by making each piece of land produce as much food as possible can so many millions earn a living on such small farms.

In both countries most of the farming people are very poor. Each family has so little land that no

Photo : Ellen Catleen

A Chinese farmer's children turning a stone roller which grinds grain into flour

matter how hard they work they get barely enough to eat, and they earn barely enough money to buy cheap cotton clothing and the few other things they need. The working people in the towns are poor, too, for they receive very low wages.

There are, of course, wealthy people in China and Japan, just as there are in other countries. But in these overcrowded Oriental lands the wealthy, and even the well-to-do people, are few in number compared with the millions of very poor.

Just suppose

1. Suppose Japan and China were much colder countries than they are. Do you think they would then be crowded lands? Give reasons for your answer.

2. Suppose they were dry lands instead of rainy lands. Do you think they would have become thickly populated? What can you say to prove that your answer is correct?

By courtesy of Nederland Line

Photo : Dorien Leigh

A distant view of two of Java's volcanic peaks, and a "close-up" of a steaming crater

JAVA AND ITS PLANTATIONS

People who have travelled all over the world will tell you that Java is one of the most interesting places they have ever visited. Java is one of the islands of the East Indies, and it belongs to the Dutch.

Map II at the front of the book will show you that Java is a mountainous island. Most of its highest mountains are volcanic peaks, like Fujiyama in Japan.

The molten lava which builds up such mountain peaks comes from bowl-shaped openings called craters. The craters are the mouths of volcanoes, which are very, very deep holes in the earth. In both Japan and Java some of the volcanoes are active, or alive. This means that from time to time clouds of steam and hot dust rise from the mountains like smoke, and streams of hot, steaming lava pour down their slopes. When this happens, people say that a volcano is erupting.

You can easily imagine what terrible damage can be done by a great volcanic eruption. The streams of hot lava pouring down the slopes destroy everything in their path. Forests in their way burst into flame. Crops and homes are destroyed, and people have to flee for their very lives.

In this way volcanoes are enemies of man, but in another way they are friends. Lava, as it cools, hardens into solid rock. This rock, when ground to fine particles by streams, makes rich soil. In all volcanic regions there is much lava soil spread over the lowlands round the bases of the mountains.

When you were reading about the Amazon and Congo basins, you learned that soils in rainy tropical lands are apt to be rather poor. Java is a rainy tropical land, and long ago it was almost entirely covered with forests, as the Amazon and Congo basins are to-day. Now, however, only about one-fifth of the island is covered with forests. Can you think why?

It is because in Java there is so much rich lava soil. This has led the people to cut down the trees over large areas to clear the land for farms and plantations.

Java is by no means wholly mountainous. Parts of it are hilly uplands not too rough for farming, and in the valleys and coastal lowlands there are good-sized stretches of level land. The lowlands, the hilly uplands, and even some of the mountain-sides are used for growing crops.

The upper map on page 11 will show you that Java is crowded with people. Both the hot, steamy lowlands and the cooler hilly parts are thickly populated. There are a number of large towns on the island, but most of the Javanese people are farmers.

Like the Japanese, the people of Java grow rice as their chief food crop. They live in villages of thatched-roofed huts surrounded by their rice-fields. The huts are half hidden in the foliage of fruit trees— tall, slender coconut - palms with feathery tops, banana trees with huge leaves, mango trees, and many others. Tropical fruits of many kinds grow so plentifully in Java that they are a regular part of the daily meals.

Photo: Frank Hurley

Native houses in a Javanese village. The tall trees are coconut-palms

Besides having fruit trees, each family has a small vegetable garden, for the Javanese flavour their rice with vegetable sauces. The soil is so rich that the farmers can feed themselves and supply most of the food needed by the people of the towns as well.

The Javanese have another and most unusual way of adding to their food-supply. In the villages nearly every family has a small fresh-water pond in the midst of the garden plot, and in the pond carp and other fish are reared for the family meals.

Photo : Dorien Leigh

Javanese farmers at work with their water-buffaloes ploughing a muddy rice-field

For work-animals the Javanese use water-buffaloes and oxen. The water-buffaloes are best for ploughing the rice-fields because their hoofs are built in such a way that they can plod about in the oozy mud and water more easily than oxen.

In visiting the native villages you will see one side of the farm life which makes it possible for so many people to live in Java. To see the other side, you will visit some of the plantations. The plantations are large farms run by companies of Europeans, but the labourers are Javanese.

Two of the most important plantation products are sugar-cane and tobacco. If you visit the sugar plantations, you will see mills where the sweet juice is squeezed out of the cane-stalks and used to make "raw" sugar. The raw sugar is sent to refineries in Britain and many other countries, and from it sugar for table use and cooking is made.

On the tobacco plantations you will see large barns where the leaves of the plants are hung up to dry and cure, so that the tobacco will have a fine flavour. When the leaves are properly cured, they are ready to be shipped away.

It happens that both sugar-cane and tobacco grow best on land such as the Javanese use for growing rice. For this reason the plantation owners rent land from the native farmers for part of each year. They hire the natives to grow the cane or the tobacco. After these crops have been harvested, the land is used by the farmers for growing their own food crops of rice.

Javanese plantation workers setting out tobacco plants

Daily work on a rubber plantation

So, you see, many of the Javanese farmers have a chance to earn money by working for the plantation companies for part of each year. The rest of the year they can devote to producing food for themselves.

In many parts of Java there are large rubber plantations. The rubber trees are set out in long, straight rows. The bark is gashed each day by native labourers, and the latex collected in buckets.

Do you remember how Piru prepares latex for shipment from his home in the Amazon forest? That is a very slow, old-fashioned way. In Java and the neighbouring lands there is a factory on every rubber plantation. In the factories latex is quickly changed by modern methods into sheets of crude rubber. In this form it is shipped away.

In the western part of Java there are many tea plantations, and in the eastern part there are many coffee plantations. For these crops the hill-sides and the lower mountain slopes are used. Many Javanese labourers are needed for picking the leaves from the tea-bushes and gathering the fruit of the coffee shrubs. Others are needed for the work connected with the preparation of tea leaves and coffee " beans ", or seeds, for shipment.

Coconut-palms grow abundantly in Java, especially on the coastal lowlands, and there are many coconut plantations. From the trees round the villages, as well as from those grown on plantations, the natives gather the big fruits. They open each coconut, take out the white " meat ", and dry it to make

A big pile of coconuts collected by a Javanese family from the trees near their house

Photo : Dorien Leigh

what is called copra. Much copra is shipped from Java to countries in the temperate zones.

You can understand now how so many people can live in Java. One reason is that the plantations provide work for thousands of people. Another, and more important reason, is that the island can be made to produce so much food. But remember that there are three things behind all this : good soils, warm weather all the year round, and plentiful rain.

Java is only one part of south-eastern Asia where plantations provide work for thousands of people. There are many sugar and tobacco plantations in the Philippine Islands ; many rubber plantations in Sumatra, the Malay Peninsula, and Ceylon ; and many tea plantations in Ceylon and India.

Perhaps you wonder why Europeans have established so many plantations in this tropical part of the world. Think how much tea and coffee are drunk in countries like Britain, and how much tobacco is smoked. Think how much sugar we use, and how much rubber we need for making tyres and other things.

Tea, coffee, rubber, and sugar-cane are crops which cannot be grown in lands as cool as Britain or the continent of Europe. Tobacco is hardier, but for the best flavour it needs much warmth. It is because Europeans and other people of the temperate zones need these and other tropical products that plantation farming is carried on in certain parts of the torrid zone.

Can you answer these questions ?

1. What do we mean when we say that Fujiyama is a volcanic peak ?
2. What harm can a great volcanic eruption do ?
3. Why are the soils round the bases of volcanic mountains often very rich ?
4. Why are the lowlands of Java better for farming than the lowlands of the Congo and Amazon basins ?
5. What are tropical plantations, and how are they different from native farms in the tropical lands ?
6. Why are there so many plantations in Java and other parts of south-eastern Asia ?
7. What would you say are the principal reasons why Java is so crowded with people ?

INDIA — LAND OF CONTRASTS

Do you know what the word " contrast " means ? It means a difference which can be clearly seen or understood. For example, there is a contrast between red and green traffic lights, because red and green are such very different colours.

It would be hard to find a country where there are greater contrasts than in India. India, you know, is part of the British Empire. It has so many millions of people that it is one of the most crowded lands of the whole world.

Map II at the front of the book will show you that the giant ranges of the Himalaya Mountains rise like a great wall above the northern plains of India. The Himalayas

Photo : Dorien Leigh

Some of the snow-capped peaks of the Himalayas as they look from a tea plantation in the foot-hills

are the highest mountains in the world. Their lower slopes are thickly forested, but their towering peaks are hidden in everlasting ice and snow.

The great stretch of lowland plains at the foot of the Himalayas is made up of the valleys of the Ganges and Brahmaputra rivers and the Punjab, which is the northern part of the Indus valley. Nowhere in the world is there a greater difference between two adjoining regions than between the snow-capped Himalayas and the low, warm plains at their base.

The Deccan, farther south, is different both from the mountains and from the northern plains. It is a hilly region, higher and rougher than the plains, but much lower

Photo : D. MacKay

Ploughing land for cotton-growing in one of the regions of lowland plains in India

Photo: Fayrer

Photo: Dorien Leigh

Another contrast—the palace of an Indian prince and the houses in a country village

and less rugged than the mountains. So, you see, there are great contrasts in the land in India.

The lower map on page 11 will show you another contrast. The Brahmaputra valley, in the eastern part of India, is one of the rainiest regions of the world. The lower part of the Indus valley, in the west, has so little rain that much of it is a desert. Notice, however, that for the most part India is a well-watered country.

If you were to spend a year in India, you would find that most of the rain comes between June and October, when south-west winds called *monsoons* blow over the country from the Indian Ocean. During those months rain falls often and in torrents. Then, rather suddenly, the rains stop, and from November to May there is a long dry season. In no other part of the world is the rainfall so unequally divided between summer and winter.

Perhaps the greatest contrasts of all in India are those which are found among the people. Many of the native princes are very wealthy, and one of them is said to be the richest man in the world. They live in beautiful palaces, cared for by scores of servants, and guarded by their own soldiers. There are a good many wealthy merchants, too.

But for every rich or even well-to-do person in India, there are hundreds of pitifully poor people. Millions of them are crowded into the towns, where they work at humble tasks for very low wages. Millions of others live on farms, where they struggle day in and day out to make a bare living.

There are, of course, very good reasons why India is such a thickly populated land. The most important reasons are the land and the weather.

Photo: W. Stokes

How cotton goes from the farms to the towns in India

To begin with, only a few parts of the country are too rough for farming, and only one part is extremely dry. For these reasons most of the land is suitable for growing crops.

Much of India, as you can see from the map, is within the tropics, and the remainder is in the warmest part of the north temperate zone. South of the Himalayas there is no part of India where the weather is ever really cold, and so farming can be carried on all the year round.

Indian farmers do much of their work by hand, but most of them have bullocks for ploughing and carting. Cattle are common all over India as work animals, but for the most part they are not reared as meat animals. The reason for this is that two-thirds of the people of India are Hindus, and Hindus will not eat beef because they regard the cow as a sacred animal.

The principal work of an Indian farmer is to grow food for his family and fodder for his cattle. In most parts of the country rice is the principal food crop, just as it is in other parts of the Orient. Other grains which are grown for food or fodder, or both, are wheat, barley, millet, and maize.

Each farmer must also produce something as a "money crop", which he can sell. The needs of a farmer and his family are not very great, but they must have a little money to buy cheap cotton clothing, tools, and other things which they cannot do without. On many farms the money crop is a small surplus of wheat or some other grain.

In parts of the Deccan and the northern plains, cotton is grown as a money crop on thousands of farms. At harvest-time the clumsy two-wheeled bullock carts rumble over the roads to the towns, piled high with big sacks of cotton.

Most of the cotton finds its way either to Bombay or Madras. These cities are seaports, and they both have large cotton mills. Part of the cotton goes to the mills, but even more is loaded in ships and sent to other countries.

97

Weaving hessian in a mill in Calcutta

In Bengal the money crop on thousands of farms is jute. Jute will remind you of Dundee, in Scotland, where so much of this fibre from India is used to make hessian, or sacking. Not all the raw jute is shipped away from India, however, for there are large jute mills in the great seaport of Calcutta.

The names of some of the money crops grown on Indian farms would sound strange to you—names such as sesamun, rape, and niger. These, and other plants such as flax and peanuts, are grown for their oily seeds. Oilseeds, as they are called, supply oil for making soap, margarine, and cooking-fat, and for many other purposes.

From the seaports of India ships carry oilseeds to Britain, Europe, and America. The growing of the plants which produce the seeds gives thousands of Indian farmers a means of making a little money.

Visitors to India are often surprised to find that in many parts of the country the farms are irrigated. At first that seems very strange, for most parts of India get a great deal of rain every year. Can you think why irrigation is necessary?

It is because most of the rain comes in the monsoon season. In many places so little rain falls during the rest of the year that the soil becomes very dry, and, if crops were not watered, they would wither and die. Many farms are irrigated with water from deep wells. Many others are irrigated from " tanks ", which are large catch-basins dug in the earth to trap the rain-water in the monsoon season.

In a good many places the government has built what are called " irrigation works ". Rivers have been dammed with concrete barrages to hold back the water in reservoirs, and canals carry the water to the farm-lands as it is needed.

Pumping irrigation water from a deep well

Photo: P. Hoefler

The "high street" of the natives in a city in India

offer for sale goods from all parts of the world.

Yet even here there are many sights to remind a visitor that he is in India, not in Europe. In the streets motor-cars, buses, and lorries weave their way in and out among slow-moving ox-carts and wandering cows. Messenger boys on bicycles speed past ragged porters pushing two-wheeled carts and barrows.

Most visitors to India see only a little of the farm-lands as they speed through them on the trains, but everyone sees something of India's crowded cities. They are full of strange and interesting sights.

In the older parts of the cities the streets are narrow and the shops are little open stalls where native merchants sit surrounded by their wares. Tiny workshops open on to the streets, too, and in them sit turbaned craftsmen making many different articles of wood, metal, leather, and ivory. Yet not far away there may be mills and factories as up-to-date as any in Britain.

In the newer parts of the cities the streets are broad and well-paved, and the buildings modern. Shops as fine as those in Europe

Indian ladies dressed in shimmering silk *saris* step out of taxi-cabs to make purchases in the shops; Indian business men in European suits, but with bright turbans wound round their heads, hurry in and out of modern banks and office buildings; and beggars in rags and tatters hold out their hands for coppers as the more fortunate folk pass by.

Photo: W. Stokes

An Indian wood-carver at work in his shop

Photo : Topical Press

Some of the strange contrasts in traffic in the crowded streets of Calcutta

Some questions about India

1. Which part of India is always cold and frozen, and why?

2. Why is most of the country warm all the year round? You should be able to give two reasons.

3. In what other ways is India well suited for farming?

4. What happens each year in the monsoon season?

5. Why do many of the farms in India have to be irrigated in spite of the heavy rains?

6. How do the farmers get water for irrigation? Remember that there is more than one way of getting it.

7. What do the Indian farmers grow chiefly as food and fodder crops?

8. What do they grow as money crops?

9. What do you think are the principal reasons why India is one of the most crowded countries in the world?

Some things to explain

1. Now that you have learned a little about India, are you ready to agree that it is a land of contrasts? If you are, explain why.

2. Name some of the products of India which come to Britain, and explain why we need them.

3. India and Canada, as you know, are both parts of the British Empire. India is only half as large as Canada, yet it has about thirty-five times as many people. How do you explain this fact?

2. THE CROWDED PART OF THE NEW WORLD

If you had been living five hundred years ago instead of now, you would never have heard the name America. In those days no one knew that there were two great continents across the Atlantic Ocean from Europe and Africa.

The time came when brave explorers crossed the Atlantic in little sailing ships and brought back word of the lands on the opposite side. At first people thought that these lands were part of eastern Asia. When it was found that they were new continents, hitherto unknown, people said that a " new world " had been discovered.

It was not long before the new continents were given their names— North America and South America; but even to-day these lands of the Western Hemisphere are still called the lands of the New World.

The upper map on page 11 will show you that there are no large areas of the New World which are as thickly populated as China, India, and western Europe. One reason for this is that only a few hundred years have passed since white people from Europe first crossed the Atlantic Ocean to make new homes in America. America would probably never have been thickly populated by the Red Indians alone.

However, as you will see from the map, there is one large area of North America which has a great many people. That area is the eastern half of the United States and the adjoining part of southern Canada.

If by now you have become a good map-explorer, you will be able to discover for yourself some of the reasons why this part of North America is thickly populated. On the next page you will find some directions which will help you.

What most visitors from Europe see first in America — the "towers of Manhattan"

Photo: Planet News

Helps for map study

1. Turn to the upper map on page 11 again. Is the thickly populated area of North America in the northern part of the north temperate zone, or in the southern part? What does that lead you to think about the weather?

2. From the lower map on the same page you can discover another important fact about the weather in the thickly populated area of North America. Has it plenty of rain, or only a little?

3. Now find the same part of North America on Map I at the front of the book. Is it mostly mountainous, or has it large stretches of plains?

4. You have discovered (*1*) that the thickly populated area of North America is in the southern, or warmer, part of the north temperate zone; (*2*) that it has plenty of rain; and (*3*) that it has large stretches of plains. Say how you think these facts work together to make it possible for so many people to live in that part of the New World.

AMERICA'S BUSY CITIES

If you were to go on a visit to the United States of America, you would probably land at the great seaport of New York. New York is a huge city, where almost as many people live as in London.

Entering the harbour of New York, you would see a sight which you would never forget. Straight ahead are the "towers of Manhattan". Manhattan is the island on which the central part of New York is situated. The "towers" are giant buildings which rise so high into the air that they are called sky-scrapers.

A twenty-storey building is low for a New York sky-scraper. Many are more than fifty storeys high, and the highest one of all has over a hundred storeys. They are used as office buildings and hotels.

Photo: Keystone

Busy Fifth Avenue, New York's leading shopping street

Photo: Keystone

Two tall blocks of New York flats

You mustn't think, though, that all the buildings in New York are sky-scrapers. There are thousands of much lower buildings, but even so, many of them still seem very high to visitors from the Old World.

This is one way in which American cities differ from cities in Britain and Europe. For the most part, business buildings and hotels are higher. Even the blocks of flats are generally higher than ours. Many are so high that lifts are not only convenient, but necessary, for the people would be worn out if they had to climb so many flights of stairs to their homes.

The higher a building is, the more people can live or work in it without using any more ground-space. So, you see, by building high into the air, the Americans pack even larger numbers of people into a small area in their cities than we do.

Just as there is no city in Britain quite like London, so there is none in the United States quite like New York. It is the largest city, the leading seaport, and the greatest business centre of the country. Many thousands of people work in its shops, hotels, business offices, and factories. Thousands of others work at the docks and quays, where ships from all over the world are always coming and going.

With so many people, there must, of course, be many means for getting about. The trams, buses, and taxi-cabs which crowd the streets can deal with only part of the traffic in this great city. Beneath the ground

Iron-works in Pittsburgh, one of America's "bee-hives of industry". The iron ore comes from mines like the one in the picture on the next page

Photo: Dorien Leigh

The suburbs are pleasant places where large numbers of people live in detached houses which are shaded by trees and separated from one another by lawns and gardens. As the suburbs become more crowded, some of the older houses are pulled down, and blocks of flats are put up on their sites.

The Americans often say that their cities are "bee-hives of industry". They mean that their cities are manufacturing centres, with many mills and factories. In that way the eastern half of the United States is like Britain and her neighbours in western Europe. These two parts of the world, facing one another across the Atlantic Ocean, supply by far the greater part of the world's manufactured goods.

In America there are several cities whose great iron-and-steel works would remind you of Sheffield and Middlesbrough. There are districts whose huge textile mills would remind you of Lancashire and the West Riding of Yorkshire. There are certain cities where more motor-cars are built and more tyres made than anywhere else in the world. There are great engineering and shipbuilding districts like Tyneside and the Clyde.

is a network of tunnels for fast electric trains like that of the Underground Railways in London. High above the streets, on what are called elevated tracks, other electric trains carry people from place to place.

There are many great cities in the eastern half of the United States, and while none of them is as large as New York, they are all busy, bustling places. Several cities on the sea-coast, besides New York, are great seaports.

Each city is ringed round with suburban towns, many of them so close together that you cannot tell where one ends and the next begins. Many of the people who live in the suburbs work in the cities. They go to and from their work in trams, buses, and trains, or in their own motor-cars.

In fact, it would be hard for you to think of anything, large or small, cheap or costly, that is not manufactured somewhere in the busy cities of America. The Americans themselves use huge quantities of these manufactured goods, but their mills and factories also turn out large surpluses of manufactures which are shipped to many different parts of the world.

Some questions to answer

1. Which part of the earth is called the New World? How did it get that name?
2. In which part of the New World is the largest area of thickly populated land?
3. Why is that area less crowded with people than western Europe?
4. In what ways are these two parts of the world alike?
5. In what ways is New York like London?
6. What do you think is the most important thing to remember about the cities in the thickly populated part of America? Why do you think so?

AMERICAN FARMS, FORESTS, AND MINES

The mills and factories of the eastern half of the United States provide work for thousands and thousands of people. That is one reason why this part of the country is so thickly populated. But behind all the manufacturing are the farms, forests, and mines of America.

Photo: Keystone
An open-pit iron-mine in America. Steam shovels dig the ore from the pit and load it into railway waggons

The farms supply huge quantities of food and certain raw materials such as cotton and wool. The forests supply lumber and pulp-wood. From the mines come coal for power, and iron, copper, lead, zinc, and other metal ores. Without these, manufacturing would be impossible.

When people from Britain and Europe first settled in what is now the eastern part of the United States, they found most of the land thickly covered with forests. There were no roads in the forests, but only the footpaths of the Red Indians.

The explorers and settlers from the Old World found the Red Indians

One of the many collieries in the valleys in the Appalachian Highlands

Photo: Keystone

scattered over nearly all parts of the two Americas — in the cold parts and the warm parts, and in the rainy parts and the dry parts. In the part of North America which is now thickly populated, the Indians were living in villages which were nothing but little clusters of rude huts. The men hunted and fished, and the women grew maize and vegetables in small clearings among the trees.

If one of the Indian chiefs could come to life to-day, he would find such great changes that he would never recognize his homeland of long ago. If he wanted to find his own people, he would have to go to scattered lands called Indian Reservations which the government of the United States has set aside for them.

Over large areas the forests where the Indians hunted have disappeared, and in their place are miles and miles of farm-lands, thickly dotted with cities and towns. Rivers which once flowed through a wilderness of trees are now bordered by motor-roads and railways and spanned by scores of bridges. The network of roads and railways which connect the cities and towns spreads over the country like a giant cobweb.

Can you think why such large areas of forests have been turned into farm-lands? Remember that the eastern half of the United States has large stretches of plains and plenty of rain. The forests, you see, covered lands which had only to be cleared of trees to be well suited for the growing of crops.

Map I at the front of the book shows that the most extensive stretch of plains in the United States is in the basin of the Mississippi River. The Mississippi Basin is one of the best farming regions in the world. The surface is generally level, the soils are fertile, and, except in the westernmost part, there is plenty of rain for crops. If you were to travel westwards from New York City into the Mississippi Basin, you would first cross the Appalachian Highlands. These are mountainous lands, and the steeper slopes are still forested, but the valleys have been cleared for farming and are dotted with towns.

If you were to explore the Appalachian Highlands, you would

Photo: Planet News

An American oil-field. Under each tall derrick there is a deep well from which petroleum is pumped

soon discover that this region is one of America's treasure-houses of mineral wealth. You would find coal-mines in many places, and oil-fields in others. Oil-fields are places where petroleum is pumped from wells which have been sunk deep down in the ground.

Petroleum is a thick, brownish-black oil. It is very useful, because it supplies us with lighter oils such as petrol and kerosene, and with fuel-oil, which is burned to make steam-power, like coal. The Americans are fortunate in having both these important fuels — coal and petroleum. There are rich coal-fields and oil-fields in several other parts of the United States besides the Appalachian Highlands.

Photo: Keystone

Two colliers at work with an electric cutting-machine in an American coal-mine

Photo: Dorien Leigh
An American farmer cultivating a huge field of young corn in the Mississippi Basin

Suppose you pretend that you have crossed the highlands, and are now in the great stretch of plains which make up the Mississippi Basin. Wherever you go, you will see rich farm-lands, and every few miles you will pass through a busy town or city.

You will find these American farm-lands different in many ways from ours in Britain. There are no small villages such as we have, for each farm-house stands in the midst of its own lands. Fields and pastures are enclosed by wire fences instead of by hedges or stone walls. But the thing which will perhaps surprise you most is the size of the farms, for they are much larger than ours.

If it is midsummer, you will see miles and miles of grain-fields where wheat, oats, or perhaps rye or barley, are fast ripening in the hot sunshine. You will also see miles and miles of corn-fields. Corn is the American name for maize. It has broad green leaves, and it grows so high that when full-grown it stands well above a tall man's head.

Then, too, you will see large pastures where dairy cows and beef cattle are feeding on clover, alfalfa, and other kinds of hay. If you stop to visit some of the farms, you will see hundreds and hundreds of pigs.

Another thing you will notice is that American farmers use more machinery in their work than our farmers do. They prepare the land for planting with ploughs that turn over six or eight furrows at a time, and with harrowing machines that follow the ploughs. They plant with machine-drills, and keep the fields weeded with machine-cultivators. They harvest almost all crops except fruits and vegetables with machines.

Many farmers keep horses for help in their work, but motor-tractors are much more common than in Britain, and far more carting is done with motor-lorries than with horse-drawn waggons.

In America there are no market days when farmers sell their products in neighbouring towns. The grain that the farmers wish to sell they cart to tall buildings, called " grain

Photo: Dorien Leigh

A harvester-thresher at work on a prairie wheat-farm in the United States

elevators ", which are built at convenient points along the railways. There it is stored until it is bought by milling companies or by merchants who ship it to distant lands.

The farmers use most of their corn and considerable quantities of other grains to feed and fatten beef cattle, pigs, and sheep. These animals go by railway to large meat-packing plants in the cities. There the animals are killed and the meat is prepared for sale.

If you go far enough west in the Mississippi Basin, you will come to the prairies, which are vast stretches of grasslands with trees only along the streams. The prairies make wonderful pastures for cattle and sheep. They are also excellent for growing wheat, and here you will find the largest wheat-farms of all.

The prairie wheat-farms are so large that all the work is done by machines drawn by motor-tractors. For harvesting, the farmers have machines called " harvester-threshers ". As they move to and fro across the fields, they cut and thresh the grain at the same time.

The cattle farms and sheep farms in the prairies are called ranches. They are very large, and some of them cover hundreds of square miles. Beef cattle reared on the ranches are sent farther east in the plains to be fed on corn and other fattening foods before being sold.

While you are in the Mississippi Basin, you will probably visit Chicago and some of the other great cities. You will soon see how closely work in these " beehives of industry " is connected with work on the farms.

Photo: Dorien Leigh

Autumn in the South brings work for many Negro pickers in the cotton-fields

They have large flour-mills and meat-packing plants, and they manufacture huge quantities of the tools, machines, tractors, and other things that farmers need.

These cities, of course, have many other mills and factories besides those connected in one way or another with farming. For example, Chicago and several other cities on the Great Lakes have huge iron - and - steel works. Iron ore for the blast-furnaces comes by boat down the lakes from mines in the hills north of the Mississippi Basin.

If you follow the Mississippi River southwards to the Gulf of Mexico, you will cross part of the broad stretch of farm - land which the Americans call the cotton belt. Farther north, the weather is too cool for cotton, but here, in the south, the weather is perfect for it. Southern farmers grow so much cotton that they supply all the cotton mills in America and have a large surplus to send to Britain and to manufacturing countries in Europe.

If you visit the South in the autumn or early winter, you will see the pickers at work in the cotton-fields. Cotton is one of the few crops harvested by hand in America, for no one has as yet invented a successful machine for this work. Many of the pickers are Negroes, for there are thousands of these dark-skinned people living in the southern part of the United States.

The South is also one of the parts of the country from which the Americans get a great deal of lumber. The southern pine forests, as they are called, cover large areas where the soils are so sandy and poor that the land is not worth clearing for farming. This is really fortunate, for, if the soils were rich, the valuable forests would long ago have been destroyed.

The United States is such a large country that it would take you months and months to see all parts of it. But the few glimpses you have had of it are enough to show you why the eastern half has so many millions of people.

Suppose we sum up the reasons. First, and most important, is the fact that there is so much land suitable for farming. In America nature has provided huge stretches of plains situated where rain is plentiful and the weather is warm enough for a great variety of crops. With so much good land for farming, there is food enough for millions of people. At present the food-supply is greater than the Americans need, and much grain and meat are shipped to other countries.

A second reason is that the United States is very rich in minerals. There is plenty of coal and petroleum to provide steam-power and electric-power for manufacturing. There is plenty of iron ore for making iron and steel. Iron and steel are the raw materials needed for making all the machinery which, in turn, is used in manufacturing goods from all kinds of raw materials.

Finally, there are the people themselves. They are mostly descendants of people from the British Isles and the countries of northern Europe. They are intelligent and energetic,

Photo : Keystone
Hauling logs out of the woods in the South

and so they have been successful in putting to good use the soils, forests, and minerals of their country.

Can you answer these questions?

These are not hard questions, but they want thinking about, and you will probably need to use your maps as helps in answering them.

1. Why is the eastern half of the United States more thickly populated than the western half?

2. Why is the Mississippi Basin more thickly populated than the Amazon Basin in South America?

3. Why haven't the forests of Canada been destroyed to the same extent as the forests of the United States?

4. Why are most of the people of Canada crowded into the southernmost part of the country?

A summary to make

Write a few sentences summing up the reasons why the eastern half of the United States is so well suited for farming and for manufacturing.

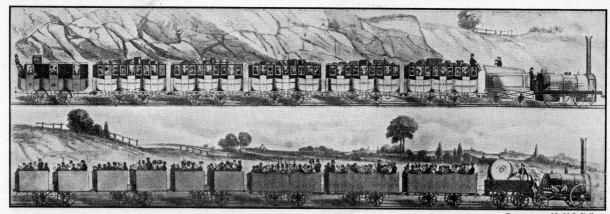

By courtesy of L.M.S. Railway

Two railway trains of about a hundred years ago. The upper one is made up of first-class carriages; the lower one of second- and third-class carriages. At their highest speed these trains could run about 30 miles an hour

3. OURSELVES AND OUR EUROPEAN NEIGHBOURS

BRITAIN: A STORY OF CHANGES

If you had been living in Britain three hundred years ago, you would have heard much talk about America and the new British settlements there. Every few weeks small sailing ships were leaving Bristol, Plymouth, and other ports, crowded with families setting out on a great adventure. They were on their way to make new homes in the New World.

It must have been very hard for the settlers to leave for ever the homes where they had been born, and to face the dangers and hardships of a new and unknown land. But like all adventurers, they had courage and perseverance, and they succeeded in what they set out to do. They made settlements in America and defended them from the Red Indians;

they turned a wilderness of forests into productive farm - lands; and they laid the foundations of a great English-speaking country in the New World.

The Britain that the settlers left behind was very different from the Britain we know to-day. It was largely a farming country, dotted with little villages and larger market towns. Then, as now, London was the largest town, but for every Londoner of those times there are more than thirty to-day.

There were no railways in the Britain of three hundred years ago, and no surfaced motor-roads. People travelled on horseback or in horse-drawn coaches. The roads were so rough that passengers in the coaches were often quite worn out with the shaking and jolting.

There were no mills and factories such as we have in Britain to-day.

Photo: Fox

How surprised the passengers in the trains of a hundred years ago would be to see our trains to-day! A powerful engine like this can pull a long line of carriages at a speed of about 90 miles an hour

Iron was smelted in small furnaces, mostly with the use of charcoal. Tools and other products of iron were hammered out by blacksmiths at their forges. Yarn was spun with the use of spinning-wheels, and cloth was woven on hand-looms in people's homes or in small workshops. Goods of all kinds were made by skilled craftsmen working with hand tools.

All this changed swiftly after some Englishmen invented machines for spinning and weaving, and a Scotsman invented the steam-engine for making power. As time went on, steam-driven machines for many different kinds of work were invented, and mills and factories were built. The craftsmen, fearing the loss of their work, fought desperately against the coming of machines, but they fought a losing fight. One machine could do the work of many hands, and do it more cheaply.

Iron ore, as you know, had been mined for hundreds of years in Britain. People had long known that coal, too, was plentiful, but until steam-engines began to be used to supply power for manufacturing, coal had been mined only in a small way. Now, because coal was needed for making steam-power, and also to supply coke for smelting, coal-mines were opened in many places.

Where coal was plentiful and could be mined easily, there the mills and factories were built, and so the coal-fields became the great manufacturing districts. Small market towns grew to be large manufacturing centres with hundreds of smoking chimneys. Blast-furnaces, built to smelt iron ore with coke, took the place of the old charcoal furnaces, and great iron-and-steel works took the place of the blacksmiths and their forges.

How ships have changed! Here you have the *Queen Mary*, and against her steel hull you see a picture of the *Bonaventure*, one of Sir Francis Drake's largest sailing ships of about three hundred and fifty years ago

This great change from hand work to machine work in factories brought many other changes with it. Many people left the farms and flocked to the towns to work as miners or factory hands. As the number of people in the country as a whole increased, the numbers living and working on farms grew less in comparison with the numbers living and working in the towns. Little by little, as more and more mills were built, Britain was transformed into the great manufacturing country which it is to-day.

Meanwhile, other important things were happening. About a hundred years ago the first railway was built, and now, as you know, the whole country is covered with a network of railways. Later came motor-cars, and the great system of surfaced highways which forms another network over the country.

On the seas, steamships and motor ships built of iron and steel have taken the place of the old wooden sailing ships, and Britain has the largest fleet of merchant ships of any country in the world. Do you know why? There are several reasons which every boy and girl ought to know.

In the first place, we are now so largely a manufacturing people that our farmers can supply only part of the food which we need. We must have ships to bring us grain, meat, and many other kinds of food from many different parts of the world.

Secondly, our mills and factories need many raw materials from other lands. We need more wool than we get from our sheep, and huge quantities of cotton, jute, and other textile fibres which we do not produce at all. We need more iron ore than we mine, and many metals, such as copper, lead, and zinc, which our country lacks. We need far more wood than our forests can supply. We must have ships to fetch these and many other raw materials from all over the world.

Thirdly, we must have ships to carry our manufactured goods to countries near and far. You can easily see why, for it is by selling the surplus products of our mills and factories that we are able to pay for our huge purchases of foods and raw materials.

Photo: Aerofilms

How do the smoking chimneys of our factories remind you of our dependence on shipping?

The products which are sent out of a country are called *exports*, and the products which are brought in are called *imports*. British ships, laden with exports of manufactured goods, leave our ports every day in the year. They return bringing the imports of food and raw materials on which our very life as a manufacturing nation depends. Our export and import trade is so great that the ships of many other nations also have a part in it.

You know, of course, that Britain is one of the crowded countries of the world. It is thickly populated chiefly because, in one way or another, manufacturing provides work for millions of people.

The mill-workers are only one of the groups of people for whom manufacturing provides work. Think of all the colliers in the coal-mines; the railway workers and the lorry drivers; the dock-workers and the seamen. Think of the thousands of clerks in business offices which handle the buying of raw materials and the selling of manufactured goods. Most of these workers, and many others, owe their chance of earning a living indirectly to manufacturing.

If Britain were still largely a farming country as it was three hundred years ago, it couldn't possibly support so many people. Without means of buying extra food from outside, it is far too small to feed so many millions.

Photo: Balogh

Contrast this picture of the **Hungarian Plain** with the picture on page 73

Do you know

1. Why iron ore was mined in Britain much earlier than coal?

2. What great change in manufacturing took place after the steam-engine was invented?

3. Why the coal-fields became the great manufacturing districts?

4. What changes the steam-engine brought about in ways of travelling on land and sea?

Some things to explain

1. We know that Britain could never have become such a great manufacturing country without its coal and iron ore. See if you can explain why.

2. We know, too, that our country would not be so thickly populated if we had not become a great manufacturing nation. See if you can explain why this is true.

3. Finally, we know that as a nation we could not get along without ships and shipping. Give what you think are the principal reasons for this.

GLIMPSES OF THE CONTINENT

Across the narrow seas from Britain lies the continent of Europe. Europe, like Britain, was well populated long before the discovery of America.

From the European countries, as from our own, people crossed the Atlantic Ocean to make new homes in the New World. The Spanish and the Portuguese settled South America, and the French made the first settlements in Canada. In what is now the United States, the French, the Germans, and the Dutch, as well as the English, made early settlements.

Perhaps you know that Europe is divided among about twenty-five different countries. The people of each country form a separate nation, and many different languages are spoken. There is not a country in the whole continent where English is the language of the people.

Photo: Paul Popper   Photo: Dorien Leigh

Differences in winter weather in Europe. At the left you see a snow-bound valley in Germany; at the right a sunny garden on the Mediterranean coast

Some of the countries are large, and some are small. Little Belgium, for example, is hardly more than one-fifth the size of England. France, on the other hand, is more than four times as large as England, and Germany is nearly as large as France.

Some day perhaps you will visit the Continent. If you do, you will discover other ways in which the various countries differ from one another. Some, such as the Netherlands and Hungary, are made up almost wholly of low, level plains. Others, such as Switzerland and Greece, are largely mountainous.

There are differences in weather, too. The northern countries have weather much like ours, with warm summers and cold winters. The Mediterranean countries are so much

farther south that their summers are very hot and their winters mild. The Mediterranean coast is so warm and sunny in winter that people from the northern countries go there to escape the cold of their own lands.

The most interesting differences are in the ways the people live and work. For example, in many of the countries the farmers do their work in modern ways just as our farmers do. But in some of the countries the farmers work in slow, old-fashioned ways. They use clumsy wooden ploughs drawn by oxen. They harvest grain by hand with sickles and scythes, and thresh it by beating or trampling the seeds off the stalks.

Look at the upper map on page 11, and you will see that in the western half of Europe there is a

Photo: Keystone

Photo: Mauritius

Old ways and new. The Romanian peasants at the left are harvesting wheat by hand; the German farmers at the right are using a harvesting-machine

large area of very thickly populated land. This crowded area extends from the North Sea and the Baltic southwards to the Mediterranean.

Let us see if we can discover some of the reasons why this part of Europe is so crowded with people. Look first at Map II at the front of the book. You will see that, while certain sections are mountainous, there are large areas of plains in western Europe. There are hilly uplands, too, but for the most part they are not too rough for farming.

Now look at the lower map on page 11. This will show you that rain is plentiful in western Europe. You see, then, that most of western Europe is well suited for farming, and that means that there is food for millions of people.

The farming people of Europe are called peasants. They are sturdy people, not afraid of hard work, and

they use their farm-land well. In France, Germany, Poland, and Czechoslovakia the peasants grow large quantities of wheat and rye for bread, and rear large numbers of cattle and pigs for meat. They grow sugar-beets for sugar, and potatoes and many other vegetables.

In the uplands of Brittany (in France), and in the Netherlands and Denmark, the cool, moist weather is especially good for dairying. In these regions so much milk is produced that there is a surplus of butter and cheese for export. You know, perhaps, that much butter from Denmark and much cheese from the Netherlands are sent across the North Sea to Britain.

Farther south, in the warmer and sunnier plains of southern France, northern Italy, Hungary, and Romania, the peasants grow a great deal of maize as well as

Photo: Herbert Felton

Photo: Paul Popper

Milking the cows on a dairy farm in the Netherlands   Picking grapes for wine

wheat. Here, too, as in the northern plains, large numbers of pigs and cattle are reared for meat.

In many parts of western Europe the hill-sides facing south are planted with vineyards. Grapes ripen splendidly on these sunny slopes, and they are used mostly for making wine. The ordinary wines of poorer quality are used by the peasants. The better wines go to the large towns or to the seaports for export. Certain French, Italian, Portuguese, and Hungarian wines are famous all over the world.

In the Mediterranean countries many fruits are grown. Among them are olives, figs, lemons, and oranges, which cannot stand frost, and also certain hardier fruits such as plums, apricots, and peaches. No doubt you have eaten oranges from Spain, olives from Italy, or figs from Greece, for large quantities of Mediterranean fruits are sold in our markets in Britain.

Wherever you go in Europe, you will find the peasants growing the crops and rearing the animals for which their land and the weather are best suited. Altogether the farm-lands of Europe produce enormous quantities of food. This is one reason why the Continent can support so many millions of people.

In addition to its fertile farm-lands, Europe is fortunate in having large stores of coal and iron ore. France has more iron ore than any country in the Old World, and Germany has rich coal-fields. Many of the other countries have smaller quantities of one or both of these very important minerals.

Photo : Brassai

The Place de la Concorde — a famous square in Paris as it looks at night

You will not be surprised, then, to find that western Europe has many busy manufacturing districts where thousands of people work in mills, factories, and mines. In northern France, Belgium, and western Germany there are large districts grimy with the smoke and dust from coal-mines, blast-furnaces, and huge ironworks. In these countries, and in certain others, there are textile-manufacturing districts as busy as ours in Britain.

Besides textiles and products of iron and steel, the mills and factories of western Europe turn out other manufactures of all kinds. It would be hard for you to think of anything which is not manufactured somewhere in Europe's many " beehives of industry ".

In a general way, the manufacturing countries of Europe carry on trade similar to ours. Their exports are chiefly manufactured goods, and their imports chiefly raw materials and foods. For them, as for us, ships and trade keep the wheels turning in the mills and factories.

In travelling in Europe you will see many fine old cities of which the people are as proud as we are of London and Edinburgh. Some people think Paris, the capital of France, is the finest city in Europe. Others choose Rome, the capital of Italy, or Berlin, the capital of Germany.

If you could fly here and there over Europe in an aeroplane, you would get a better picture of the Continent than in any other way. You would look down on carefully tilled farm-lands dotted with peasant villages, busy market towns, and crowded cities. In many places you would see the smoke rising from hundreds of factory chimneys. You would see the giant web of railways and roads which covers the land, connecting all the cities and towns.

Along all the sea - coasts you would see the busy ports with their miles and miles of docks and quays. You would see the ships which are always coming and going, carrying on trade between Europe and all parts of the world.

If we take western Europe as a whole, it is rather like the eastern half of the United States. It has very large areas of good farm-lands situated in a part of the north temperate zone where the yearly rainfall is plentiful and the weather is warm enough for a great many different kinds of crops. It has much coal and iron ore, which more than anything else have made possible its great manufacturing industries. It has a very long sea-coast dotted with ports which serve as gateways between the land and the sea, handling the great flow of exports and imports.

Western Europe, like Britain and the eastern United States, is thickly populated because it is a part of the world where nature has given man great gifts of soil, rain, and mineral wealth to work with. It is more crowded than the eastern United States because it is part of the Old World, where civilized people have been living much longer than in the New World across the sea.

Photo: Paul Popper

A glimpse of the harbour of Hamburg, Germany. Hamburg is one of the great seaports of Europe

Just suppose

1. Suppose western Europe had as little rain as the Kirghiz Steppe. Would it have more people than it has now, or fewer people? Why?

2. Suppose all of western Europe were as mountainous as Switzerland. Do you think it could support as many people as it does now? Give reasons for your answer.

3. Suppose western Europe were in the tropics. Would its lowland plains be as thickly populated as they are now? Say why you think they would, or would not.

4. Suppose western Europe were situated within the north polar cap. What effect would that have on the number of people it could support, and why?

Some things to do

1. Write a short summary saying why western Europe is fortunate in its situation, its surface, and its weather.

2. Explain the difference between exports and imports.

3. Explain why the exports of western Europe are chiefly manufactures, and why the imports are chiefly foods and raw materials.

Some Things to Remember about the Crowded Lands

You have learned that there are three parts of the world where large stretches of land are crowded with millions of people : (1) eastern and south-eastern Asia ; (2) western Europe and the British Isles ; and (3) the eastern half of the United States of America.

You can see from the upper map on page 11 that, large as these areas are, they by no means make up half, or even a fourth, of the lands of the earth. Yet in these crowded lands live three-fourths of all the world's people.

You are ready now to sum up the reasons for this very uneven distribution of people over the earth. First let us think how we account for the thinly populated parts of the world. Some, you will remember, are too hot and some are too cold. Some are too rainy and some are too dry. Some are too high and mountainous to have many people.

The cold lands cannot be used for farming. Neither can the dry lands, except in the scattered spots where there is water for irrigation. So, in the cold lands and the dry lands, the food supply is too small for large numbers of people.

The hot, rainy lands of the tropics can be made to produce food, but they are unhealthy lands, especially for white people. In the mountainous lands only the valleys can be used for farming, and so, for the most part, such lands cannot support very large populations.

So, in one way or another, very great areas of the earth are either unattractive or unsuitable as homelands for large numbers of people. They are lands where nature has not been generous in offering man opportunities for making a living.

When you think of the crowded lands, remember that they are the lands where opportunities for making a living are greatest. Their farms, forests, mines, and factories provide work for millions of people. But don't forget that of all nature's gifts in these regions, good land and weather for farming are the most precious, because food is the greatest need of all mankind.

GENERAL QUESTIONS

Some questions about continents

1. How many continents are there?

2. Use the upper map on page 11 to prove that you can name each one of the populated continents without making a mistake.

3. What is the name of the seventh continent, and where is it situated?

4. Why hasn't that continent any people?

5. Which continent is a dominion of the British Empire?

6. In which continent is the Dominion of Canada?

7. In which continent is India?

Some questions about oceans

1. What are the names of the four great oceans of the earth?

2. Which one would you cross in going from Britain to the United States of America?

3. Which one would you cross on a trip from China to Canada?

4. Which one would you cross in going from South Africa to Australia?

5. Which ocean is situated in the Far North?

6. Why isn't that ocean used by large numbers of ships, as the other three are?

A drawing to make

1. Draw a good-sized circle to represent the earth.

2. Draw lines to represent the Equator, the tropics of Cancer and Capricorn, and the Arctic and Antarctic circles. Print the names of these lines in the correct places.

3. Add two dots for the North Pole and the South Pole, and print the name of each one in the proper place.

4. Compare your drawing with the maps on pages 22-23 to see if it is correct in every way.

Some things to explain

1. On the drawing which you have just made, point out the torrid zone and explain what that name means.

2. Explain how it happens that there are cool lands, and even cold lands, in the torrid zone.

3. Point out on the drawing the two polar caps. Explain why it is that even the lowlands in these parts of the earth are cold lands.

4. Point out the north temperate zone and the south temperate zone.

5. Many people think that these two zones are the best parts of the world in which to live. Do you agree with this? Explain why you do, or why you do not.

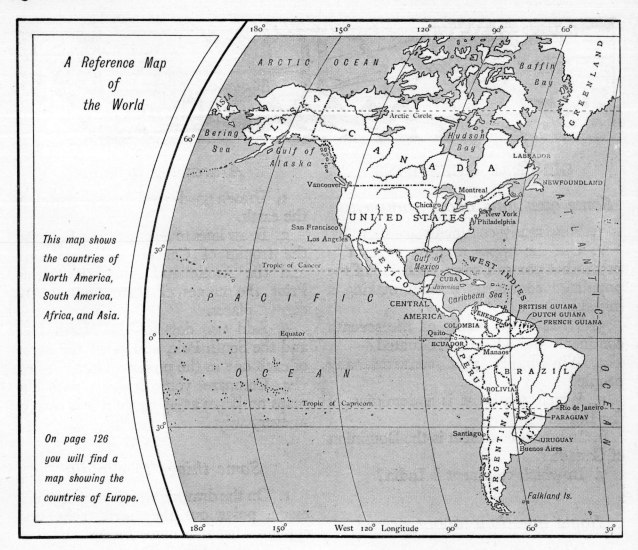

A Reference Map
of
the World

This map shows
the countries of
North America,
South America,
Africa, and Asia.

On page 126
you will find a
map showing the
countries of Europe.

The cold lands

1. Point out on this map some parts of the world which are too cold to have many people.

2. Explain why most of the people of the lands beyond the Arctic Circle are nomads.

3. Explain how the people of the northern forests make their living.

4. Give what you think are the principal reasons why neither the tundra nor the northern forests will ever be very thickly populated.

The warm, rainy lands

1. Point out on the map some rainy lands which are always warm.

2. How do the people of the tropical forests in Africa and South America make their living?

3. Why are the settlements in these forests widely scattered?

4. Why aren't these tropical lowlands thickly populated like the rainy lowlands in the temperate zones?

5. Where in the warm, rainy lands are there many plantations, and why?

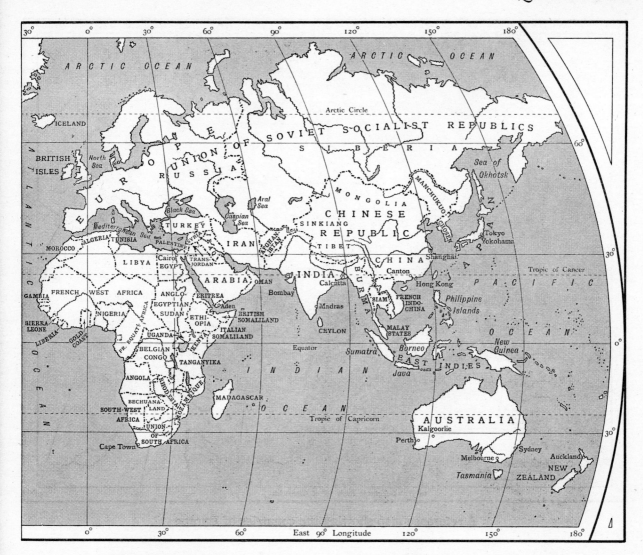

The dry lands

1. Point out on the map the lands which are too dry to have a great many people.

2. Describe the life of the nomads in the dry lands of Asia and Africa.

3. Explain why certain spots in the deserts are crowded with people.

4. Where in Africa is there a long, narrow oasis, and why?

5. Do you think the dry lands will ever be much more thickly populated? Give reasons for your answer.

The crowded lands

1. Point out on the map the three parts of the world where large areas of land are crowded with people.

2. Explain as fully as you can why each of these areas can be made to produce large quantities of food.

3. Two of these areas are the greatest manufacturing regions of the world. Which two are they?

4. What minerals has nature given these areas which have helped them to become manufacturing regions?

125

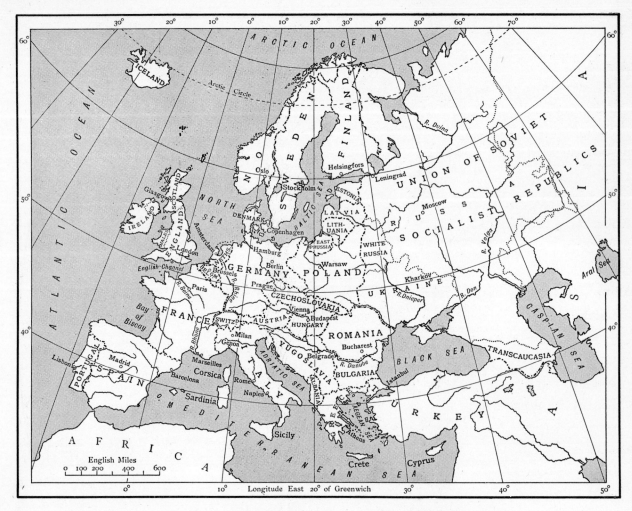

A reference map showing the countries of Europe

Getting cargoes for ships

See if you can name one or more countries where a ship might be sent to get each of these cargoes. As you name each country, point it out on the map on pages 124-125.

Raw cotton   Tea
Rubber   Wheat
Meat   Raw silk
Jute   Lumber
Rice   Furs
Palm kernels   Tobacco
Butter and cheese   Wood-pulp

A suggestion for a play

Would you and the other children in your class like to give a geography play? If you would, divide yourselves into four or five groups: one group for each act of the play.

The children of each group may choose some far-away land and pretend that they are the people living there. The fun of the play will be to see how well you and the other pupils in your group can represent the life of the people in the region you have chosen.

INDEX

Africa
  Congo Basin 63, 64, 68–72
  Nile Oasis 43
  Sahara Desert 40, 41
America – see Canada, North America, South America, United States of America
Antarctica 13–19
Antarctic Circle 22
Arctic Circle 22
Asia – see also China, India, Japan
  Ceylon 94
  Iran, Tarim Basin, and Desert of Gobi 41
  Kirghiz Steppe 35–40
  Malay Peninsula 94
  northern forest (Siberia) 50, 54, 55, 56
Australia
  black-fellows 47–48
  gold-mining 49

Britain 112–116

Canada
  fur-trapping 5–8, 52–56, 59
  northern forests 5–8, 50, 59–61
  tundra 31
China 82, 87–89

Deserts 40–45, 47–48, 50

East Indies – see Java
Equator 15–16
Eskimos 30–33

Eurasia 50
Europe 116–121
  farming 117–119
  logging 56–59
  manufacturing 119–121
Exports 115

Farming 37, 43, 70, 74, 78, 83–86, 89, 91–94, 97–98, 105, 106, 108–109, 110–111, 117–119
Fishing 25, 31–33, 65, 69
Forests
  northern 5–8, 50–61
  tropical 63–72
Frigid Zones
  north 23
  south 22
Fur-trapping 5–8, 52–56, 59

Greenland 24

Herding 25–29, 30–31, 34, 35–40, 41, 75
Hunting 31–33, 65, 69

Imports 115
India 94, 95–100
Irrigation 44, 48, 98

Japan 82–86
Java 90–94

Kirghiz 35–40

Lapps 25–30
Logging (lumbering) 56–61
London 8–10

Manufacturing 86, 88–89, 104–105,
    112–116, 119–121
Maps
    Antarctica 14
    Antarctica compared with Europe 18
    Eastern Hemisphere 23
    Europe 126
    population of world 11
    rainfall of world 11
    Western Hemisphere 22
    World 124, 125
Mining 49, 59, 78, 105, 107, 113, 120
Monsoons 96
Mountainous Lands 73–79

North America
    deserts 48, 49
    fur-trapping 52–56, 59
    northern forests 50, 59–61
    Rocky Mountains 76–77
    tundra 30–33
    United States 101–111
North Pole 14

Oases 42–45
Orient 81–100

Philippine Islands 94

Red Indians 48, 65, 105–106
Rice 83–85, 89, 91, 97
Rubber 66–67, 93

Scott, Captain 13–15
South America
    Amazon Basin 63–67, 70–72
    Andes Mountains 74–75
South Pole 14
Steppes 36–40

Temperate Zones 77
Torrid Zone 62
Tropics
    Cancer 62
    Capricorn 62
Tundra 24–33

United States of America
    Appalachian Mountains 107
    farming, mining 105–111
    Mississippi Basin 107–110
    New York 102–104
    petroleum 107

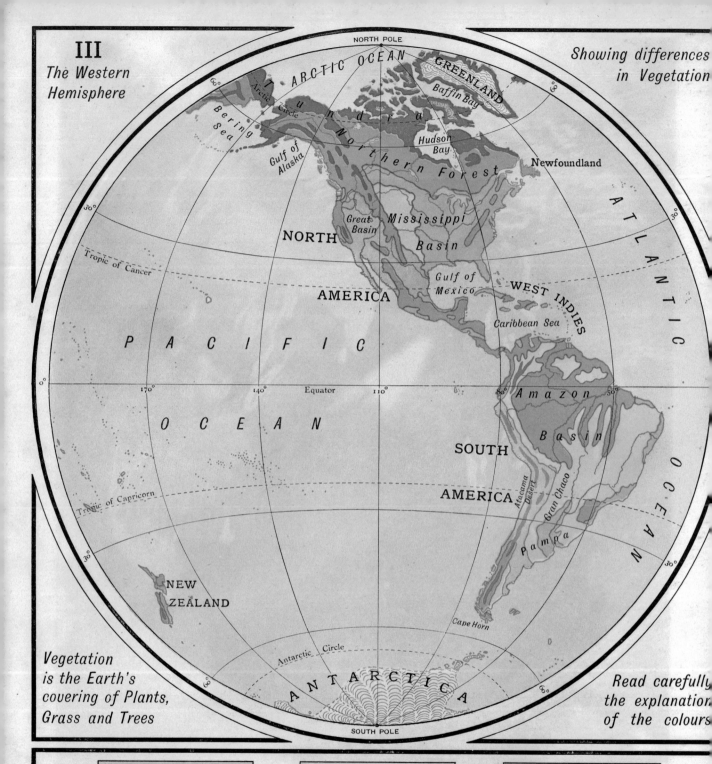

III
The Western Hemisphere

Showing differences in Vegetation

NORTH POLE

ARCTIC OCEAN

GREENLAND

Baffin Bay

Arctic Circle

Tundra

Bering Sea

Gulf of Alaska

Northern Forest

Hudson Bay

Newfoundland

NORTH

Great Basin

Mississippi Basin

Tropic of Cancer

AMERICA

Gulf of Mexico

WEST INDIES

Caribbean Sea

PACIFIC

OCEAN

Equator

Amazon

Basin

SOUTH

AMERICA

Atacama Desert

Gran Chaco

Pampa

Tropic of Capricorn

NEW ZEALAND

Cape Horn

Antarctic Circle

ANTARCTICA

SOUTH POLE

ATLANTIC OCEAN

Vegetation is the Earth's covering of Plants, Grass and Trees

Read carefully the explanation of the colours

Deserts and Poorer Steppes	Better Steppes, Prairies, and Savannas	Cultivated Land, Grass, and Woodland
These are the driest lands. Some are sandy; some are rocky; and others have scattered patches of grass. Only in the oases are there any trees.	*These are grasslands, used mostly for grazing. The steppes and prairies have trees only along the streams. The savannas are tropical grasslands with scattered trees.*	*These are lands which are used mostly for farming. The parts which are not cultivated, or farmed, are covered with grass or woods.*